THE KEY

STUDENT STUDY GUIDE

nguage Arts 6

THE KEY

THE KEY series of student study guides is specifically designed to assist students in preparing for unit tests, provincial achievement tests, and diploma examinations. Each ***KEY*** includes questions, answers, detailed solutions, and practice tests. The complete solutions show problem-solving methods, explain key concepts and highlight potential errors.

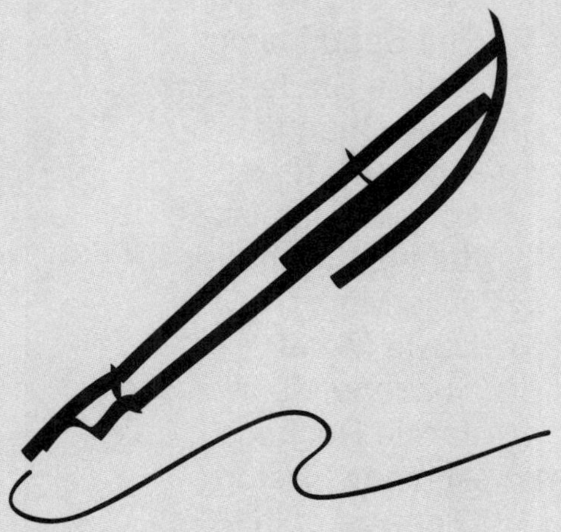

Reading

Listening

Viewing

Writing

Speaking

Representing

Canadian Cataloguing in Publication Data

Rao, Gautam, 1961–
THE KEY – Language Arts 6

1. Language Arts – Juvenile Literature. I. Title

Published by:
Castle Rock Research Corp
2340 Manulife Place
10180–101 Street
Edmonton, AB T5J 3S4

5 6 7 FP 07 06 05

Printed in Canada

Publisher
Gautam Rao

Editors
Mun Prasad
Shirley Wacowich

Contributors
Jennifer Heath
Kerry Light
Anthony Regan
Carol Strilchuk

Print Production
Phil Beauchamp
Alesha Braitenbach
Nishi Chadha
Mark Chan
Lorraine James
James Kropfreiter
Julie May
David Moret
Suzanne Morin
Jackie Pacheco
Abhinav Rastogi
Diana Seguin
Jan Witwicky
Gary Yaremchuk

Castle Rock Research Corp

Dedicated to the memory of Dr. V. S. Rao

THE KEY – Language Arts 6

THE KEY for Language Arts 6 is specifically designed to assist students who are preparing to write the provincial achievement test. The goal is to prepare students for all aspects of the exam by providing useful information on the two parts of the Provincial Achievement Test, Part A - *Writing* and Part B - *Reading*. Each section has been analyzed to gain a strong understanding of the critical elements being assessed. Based upon this analysis, guidelines for approaching each element of the provincial achievement test have been developed. The strategies and suggestions presented here are intended to be used in conjunction with the curriculum concepts that students have studied in the classroom.

THE KEY is organized into the following sections.

I **Key Tips for Being Successful at School** provides students with examples of study and review strategies. Information is included on learning styles, study schedules, and developing review notes.

II **Writing** shows students how to compose, organize, structure, and express their writing. Students will become familiar with what to expect on the provincial achievement test. They will learn how to make their writing more precise, descriptive, and grammatically correct.

III **Reading** provides strategies for understanding fiction, poetry, and visual texts. Students learn what to do before, during, and after reading their selections. The section also includes suggestions for how to complete a reading test.

IV **Key Strategies for Success on Tests** explores topics such as common exam question formats and strategies for responding, directing words most commonly used, how to begin the exam, and how to manage test anxiety.

V **Provincial Achievement Tests** includes the 2000 and 2001 Provincial Achievement Tests. Students may use these previously administered achievement tests to become familiar with the format and rigor of the exam. **Detailed solutions** are provided for each question. Solutions examine all four choices and explain why the correct answer is the most suitable response.

THE KEY *Study Guides* are available for Language Arts 6, Mathematics 6, Science 6 and Social Studies 6. A complete list of the ***THE KEY*** *Study Guides* for Grades 3 to 12 is included at the back of this book.

For information about any of our resources or services, please call Castle Rock Research Corp at 780.448.9619 or visit our web site at http://www.castlerockresearch.com.

At Castle Rock Research we strive to produce a resource that is error free. If you should find an error, please contact us so that future editions may be corrected.

CONTENTS

KEY Tips for Success on Tests

Provincial Achievement Tests

Answers and Solutions

NOTES

KEY TIPS FOR BEING SUCCESSFUL AT SCHOOL

NOTES

KEY TIPS FOR BEING SUCCESSFUL AT SCHOOL

DOING YOUR BEST AT SCHOOL

There are some things that you can do to help you do your best at school. Here are a few ideas that may help you to feel more successful at school.

- **ATTEND SCHOOL REGULARLY** so you do not miss any lessons, notes, and important activities that help you learn.
- **KEEP A POSITIVE ATTITUDE.** Always look at what you can already do and what you already know.
- **BE PREPARED TO LEARN.** Have the necessary pencils, pens, notebooks and other materials in class.
- **COMPLETE ALL OF YOUR ASSIGNMENTS.** If the assignment or question is difficult for you, work it through as far as you can so your teacher can see exactly where you are having difficulty.
- **SET SMALL GOALS** for yourself when you are learning new material. For example, in learning the multiplication facts, do not try to do it all in one night. Work on only one set of facts each study session. When you have memorized that set, move on to another one until you have memorized all the multiplication facts from 1 to 12.
- **REVIEW YOUR CLASSROOM WORK** regularly at home to be sure you understand the material you learned in class.
- **ASK YOUR TEACHER FOR HELP** when you do not understand something or are having a difficult time completing your assignments.
- **GET PLENTY OF REST AND EXERCISE.** Concentrating in class is hard work. You need to be well rested and have a chance to play with your friends. This helps you to keep a positive attitude about your school work.
- **EAT HEALTHY MEALS.** A balanced diet keeps you healthy and gives you the energy you need for studying at school and at home.

KNOWING HOW YOU 'LEARN BEST'

Every student has a certain manner in which it seems easier for him or her to learn. The manner in which you 'learn best' is called your learning style. By knowing your best method of learning, you can increase your success at school. Most students use a combination of learning styles. Do you know what type of learner you are? Read the following descriptions. Which of these common learning styles do you use most often?

- You may be an ***auditory learner*** (sometimes called a *linguistic* learner) if you learn best by saying, hearing and seeing words. This type of learner is good at memorizing things such as dates, places, names and facts.
- You may be a ***visual learner*** (sometimes called a *spatial* learner) if you learn best by seeing and working with pictures. This type of learner is good at puzzles, visualizing things, and reading maps and charts.
- You may be a ***kinesthetic learner*** if you learn best by touching, moving, and figuring things out using manipulatives. This type of learner is good at physical activities and learns through movement.

(Adapted from http://snow.utoronto.ca/Learn2/mod3/mistyles.html)

Your learning style may not fit "cleanly" into one specific category but may be a combination of two or more styles. Knowing your learning style allows you to organize your study notes in a manner that provides you with the most meaning. For example, if you are:

- an ***auditory learner***, you may need **to write and then "say out loud"** the steps in a process, the formula, or actions that lead up to a significant event;
- a ***visual learner***, you may need to use strategies like **mind mapping and webbing** to organize your information and study notes;
- a ***kinesthetic learner***, you may need to **draw your finger over a diagram** to remember it, or to **"tap out" the steps** in solving a problem, or "feel" yourself writing or typing the formula.

MAKE TIME TO STUDY

A study schedule helps you to manage your time. It may help you to organize your time so that you can complete your assignments on time and do your best to prepare for unit tests and year-end exams.

You should review your class notes regularly. Reviewing your notes helps you to learn and remember the new ideas and concepts. Depending on the grade you are in, you should spend 15 to 30 minutes each evening reviewing your work.

To make the most effective use of your study time, you should try to:

- study at the same time every day
- study in the same quiet spot
- start with the subject that you find most difficult or challenging
- use your learning-style strategies in your review

KEY TIPS FOR REVIEWING

You may find some of the following tips helpful when reviewing your notes during your study time.

STUDY NOTES

MIND MAPPING OR WEBBING

- Write the key word, idea, or formula in the middle of your page.
- Write other related ideas on your page and link them together using lines.
- Use coloured markers, numbering, or underlining to show the most important ideas.

The following is an example of a mind map or web that you might use in Language Arts when you are writing a story.

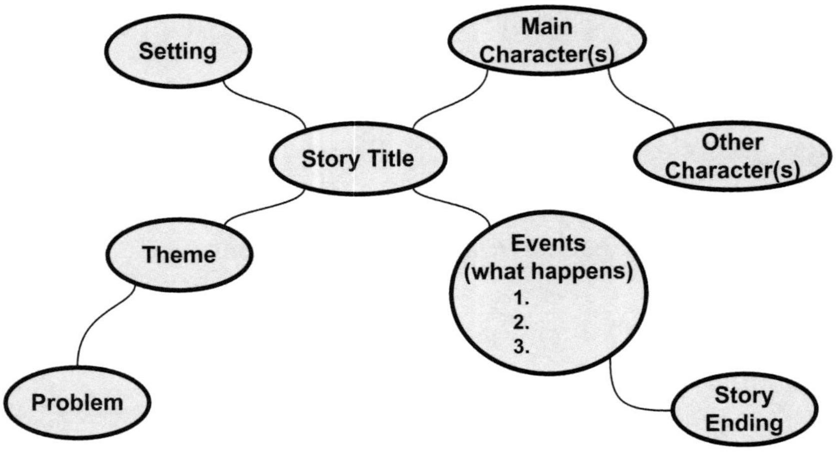

CHARTS

- Use charts to organize your information. A chart is like a picture; it shows you all of the information at one time.

The following two examples of charts can help you to remember important information and relationships between some of the metric units of measurement.

Units of Measurement	
Base quantity	**Unit**
Length	centimetre (cm), metre (m), kilometre (km)
Weight	milligrams (mg), gram (g), kilogram (kg), tonne (t)
Capacity	millilitre (mL), litre (L)

Converting Units of Measurement		
Length	**Capacity**	**Weight**
1 cm = 10 mm	1 000 mL = 1 L	1 kg = 1 000 g
1 m = 100 cm		1 t = 1 000 kg
1 000 m = 1 km		

INDEX CARDS

- Write a key word or question on one side of the index card.
- On the reverse side, write the definition of the word, answer to the question, or any other important information that you need to remember.

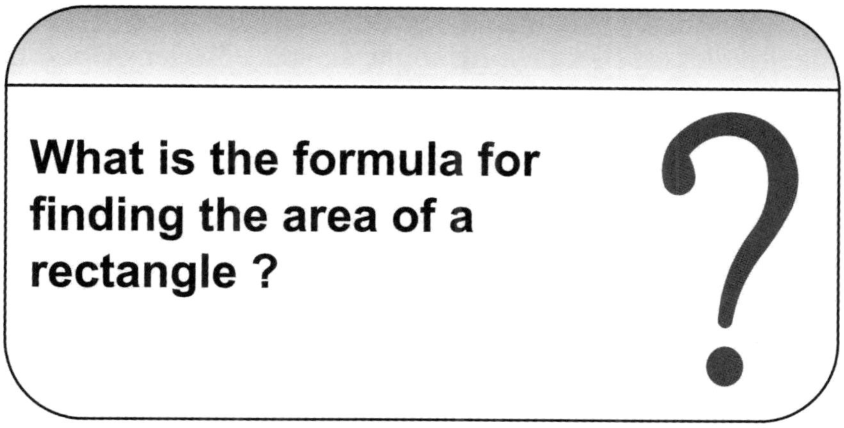

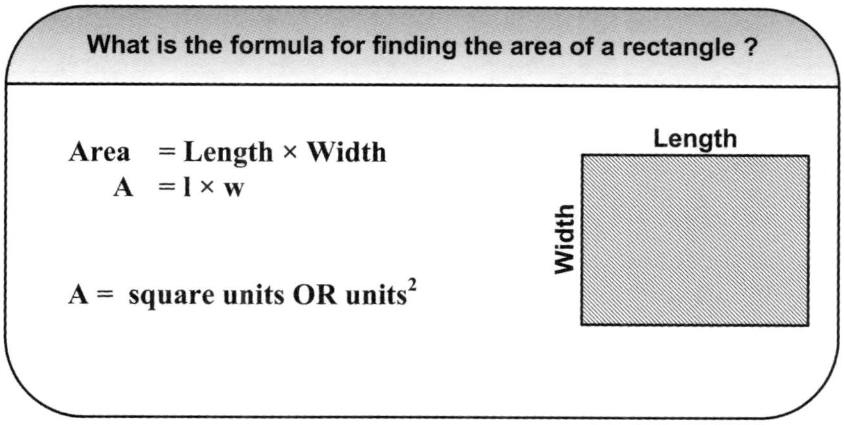

SYMBOLS

- Use symbols to mark your class notes. For example, an exclamation mark (!) might point out something that "must be learned well" because it is a very important idea. A question mark (?) may identify something you are not certain about, and a diamond (◊) or asterisk (*) may identify interesting information that you want to remember. A check mark (✓) or an × can be used to show that you agree or disagree with the statement, sentence, or paragraph.

MEMORIZING

- **ASSOCIATION** relates new learning to something you already know. For example, in remembering the spelling of 'dessert' and 'desert', you know 'sand' has only one 's' and so should desert.
- **MNEMONIC DEVICES** are sentences you create to remember a list or group of items. For example, the first letters of the words in the sentence "**E**very **G**ood **B**oy **D**eserves **F**udge" helps you to remember the names of the lines on the treble clef staff (E, G, B, D, and F) in music.
- **ACRONYMS** are words formed from the first letters of the words in a group. For example, **HOMES** helps you to remember the names of Canada's five Great Lakes (**H**uron, **O**ntario, **M**ichigan, **E**rie, and **S**uperior).
- **VISUALIZING** requires you to use your mind's eye to "see" the chart, list, map, diagram, or sentence as it is in your textbook, notes, on the board, computer screen or in a display.

KEY STRATEGIES FOR SUCCESS – A CHECKLIST

Review, review, review. That's a huge part of doing well at school and preparing for tests. Here's a checklist for you to see how many suggested strategies for success you are using. Read each question and then put a check mark (√) in the correct column. Look at the questions where you have marked the 'No' column. Think about how you might try using some of these strategies to help you do your best at school.

KEY Strategies for Success	Yes	No
Are you going to school regularly?		
Do you know your learning style – how you learn best?		
Do you spend 15 to 30 minutes a day reviewing your notes?		
Do you study in a quiet place at home?		
Do you clearly mark the most important ideas in your study notes?		
Do you practice answering multiple choice, numerical response, essay and written response questions?		
Do you ask your teacher for help when you need it?		
Are you maintaining a healthy diet and sleep routine?		
Are you participating in regular physical activity?		

WRITING

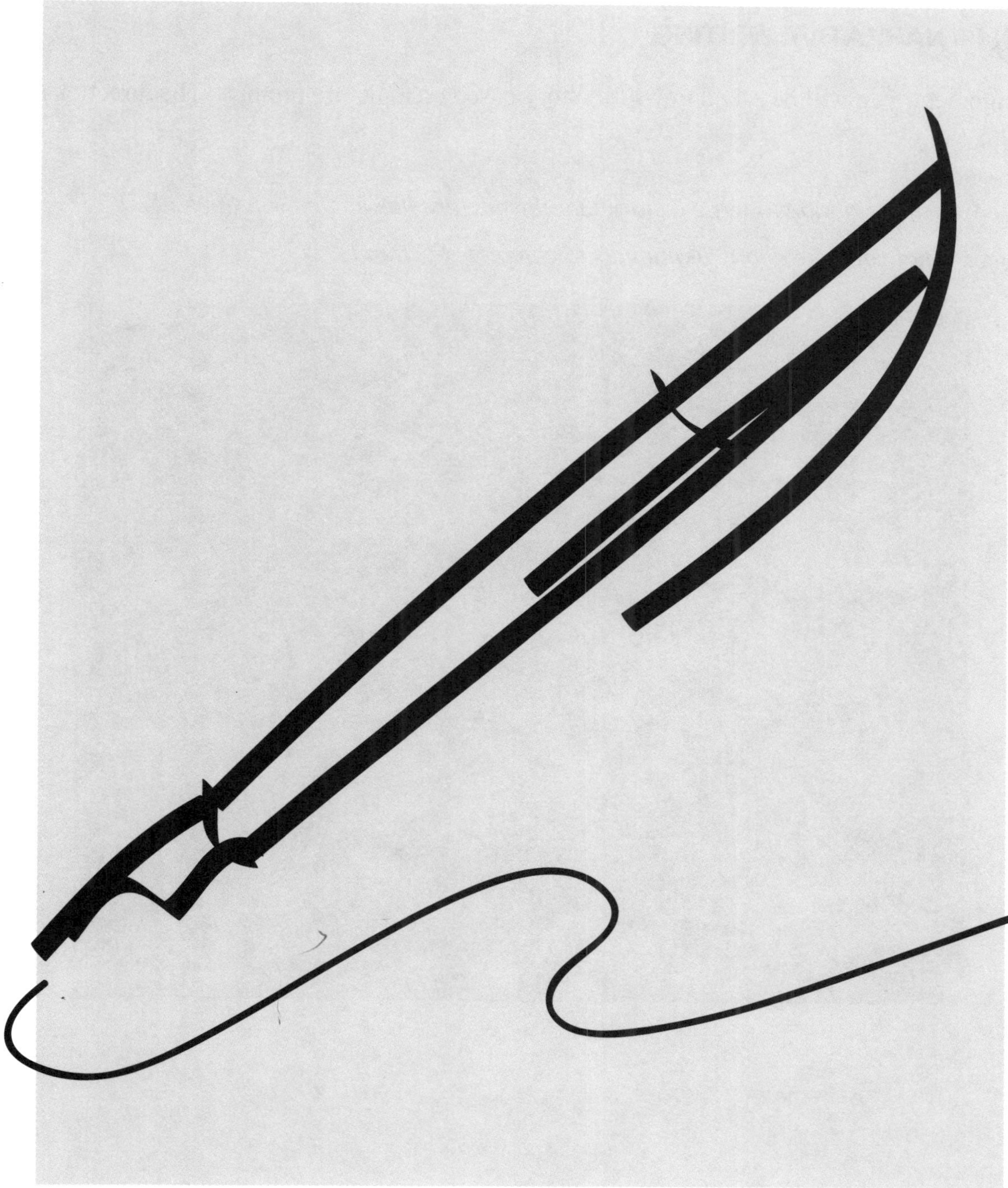

Part A: Writing

The writing section of the Grade 6 English Language Arts Provincial Achievement Test requires you to complete two assignments. Section I asks you to respond to a picture by writing a story. Section II requires you to complete a written assignment to fulfill a specified purpose. Part A of ***THE KEY*** has been organized to help you to prepare for both assignments.

SECTION I – NARRATIVE WRITING

In this assignment, you will be asked to write a story based on a picture prompt. The directions will look like this:

> *Use your imagination to write a story that this picture has helped you think about. We suggest that you take about 70 minutes to complete Section I.*

When writing your story, you should be sure to

a) **consider** your audience

b) **focus** on your purpose

c) **organize** your thoughts appropriately in sentences and paragraphs

d) **use vocabulary** that is interesting and descriptive

e) **edit** your work directly on your writing

f) **budget** your time

It may be helpful to consider the following questions when you are planning your story.

1. What are the notable features of the picture prompt? In the example on page 10, you might have noticed the following details:

- a person crawling into a dark cave
- a soccer ball
- the notebook that the girl is carrying
- the clothing that the characters are wearing
- the ivy growing on the wall

2. What does the picture and its features remind you of or make you think about? In the example, you might be reminded of:

- an adventure you once took with your younger sister
- a creepy story you once heard
- walking home from school

3. What type of story would you like to write for this picture prompt? Based on this example, you might write:

- an exciting adventure
- a fantasy story filled with suspense
- an eerie mystery
- a heartfelt drama

4. When and where will your story take place? Your story can take place in more than one location and/or more than one time period. For example, you might decide to have your story take place

- in the present
- in the past
- in the future
- at night
- in your own city
- in a foreign country
- in an imaginary place
- in a playground
- in a crowded area

5. Who will your main character(s) be? In this example, the main character(s) might be

- a young person
- a rich person
- an alien
- a detective
- someone who is famous

6. What problem(s) will your character(s) face? Some possible conflicts are

- character versus character (a conflict between two people or things)
- character versus nature (a character's struggle to survive against the elements of nature)
- character versus society (a conflict between a main character and a societal rule, belief, or system)
- character versus self (a character's internal struggle that tests his or her ability to cope)

7. How will the story end?

- Will the events of the story result in a character's change of heart or way of thinking?
- Will the ending bring closure to all parts of the story or leave some unanswered questions?
- Is the ending a logical conclusion or is it an unexpected one?

8. Will your story have a theme? Some examples of possible themes are

   - love conquers all
   - good triumphs over evil
   - kindness is the best gift one can give or receive
   - friendship is more important than popularity
   - through struggle, we gain
   - hard work always pays off
   - working together is better than working alone

9. Will you state the theme of the story directly or will it be implied? If the theme is implied, it will be up to the reader to figure out the theme based on the events and details in the story.

NARRATIVE WRITING SUGGESTIONS

1. The most important goal is to communicate clearly so that the reader will understand what you are trying to say.

2. Keep your writing focused on creating a *narrative* response. Remember that your story should include a beginning, a middle, and an end.

3. Organize your work. You should have at least three paragraphs: one for the beginning, one for the middle, and one for the ending. This is only a minimum; you can always have more than three paragraphs.

4. When appropriate, use vocabulary that is interesting and descriptive. Try to be creative. Make your story interesting to the reader.

5. Edit your work directly on your writing. Do not worry that this will appear messy. Watch for sentence structure, paragraphing, capitalization, punctuation, and spelling. You may want to consider double-spacing your writing so that it is easier to edit.

6. Manage your time so that you will finish the assignment. You should aim to spend about 10 minutes planning, 50 minutes writing, and 10 minutes editing your story. If time permits, re-read your story as a final check for meaning and clarity.

7. Remember to find some way to include the scene from the picture prompt in your story. You might include it at the beginning or place it closer to the end. What is important is that you include it.

HOW THE NARRATIVE WRITING WILL BE GRADED

Written assignments in Section I are graded using the following criteria.

1. **Content**: The response is plausible and uses ideas and events that are appropriate for the assignment. The response should establish a context using specific details and hold the reader's interest.

2. **Organization**: The response is organized effectively and coherently to produce a unified composition that achieves its purpose. The story should be effectively introduced and concluded.

3. **Sentence Structure**: A variety of sentence types and structures are used to achieve clarity, interest, and emphasis.

4. **Vocabulary**: Students use specific words and expressions accurately and effectively to communicate to the audience and to achieve their purpose.

5. **Conventions**: Students communicate clearly by adhering to appropriate spelling, punctuation, capitalization, and grammar conventions. The number of errors in the story will be considered in relation to the length and complexity of the response.

Content and organization are weighted to be worth twice as much as each of the other criteria.

DEVELOPING YOUR NARRATIVE

1. Content

a) Generating Story Ideas

It is important to decide what will happen in your story and why. Before you begin writing, think about the follow questions.

What is your topic? That is, what are you writing about? A mysterious event? Your feelings? An adventure?

What is your purpose? That is, why are you writing? To describe? To explain? To tell?

Who is your audience? That is, who is going to read this? Your friends? Your teacher? Other adults?

Sometimes generating a lot of story ideas helps you begin to make decisions about possible characters, events, and lessons learned. You may want to consider the following two strategies for generating ideas.

Brainstorming
Brainstorming is the technique of writing down all of your ideas without judging them. Once you have several ideas written down, you should eliminate the weaker ideas and keep only those ideas that you think might be the basis for a good story.

Asking Questions
Asking questions will help you generate many ideas for your story. Consider this set of questions when responding to a picture prompt:

- What is happening in the picture?
- What character struggle might someone in this picture be facing?
- What kind of characters do I want to write about?
- What type of story do I want to create (drama, mystery, adventure, etc)?
- What events will I focus on?
- How might the story end?
- Will a character change in any way because of a problem he/she faces?
- How will I describe the setting?
- How will I describe the characters and their behaviours?

b) Perspective (Point of View)

There are many perspectives, or points of view, from which you can tell your story. You may want to consider the following three options.

- *First Person*

When you tell your story from the first-person perspective, the main character tells the story using "I." Using this perspective allows you to include details about the thoughts and feelings of one character only.

- *Third Person*

When you tell your story from the third-person perspective, you become the narrator of the story. All characters are referred to as "he" or "she." Using this perspective allows you to include details about the thoughts and feelings of many characters.

- *An Unusual Perspective*

Sometimes writing your story from an unusual perspective can lead to an innovative story. For example, in a picture prompt that shows a bear hidden in bushes near a campsite, you could write about a family's encounter with the bear. However, instead of writing from the perspective of a family member, you could write as though you were the bear. By "becoming" the bear, you provide the reader with a surprising and unique perspective on the events of the story.

c) Story Structure

Every story starts with an idea. When you are planning your story, keep your mind open to all kinds of ideas. At the same time, you should spend some time outlining your story structure so that when you are ready to write, you can step right into it. Your outline should include the following elements:

Main Character(s)—who is in the story

Setting—when and where the story takes place

Problem—what conflict occurs in the story

Plot—the order of events in the story

Solution—how the problem is solved

Theme—the lesson of the story

Remember that your ideas and events should make sense together. You should also include enough details to captivate and maintain the reader's attention.

2. Organization

Once you have your ideas for the story structure, you need to organize them so that the story develops logically. Narratives should develop specific and detailed connections between story events and character reactions (character change, lessons learned, etc.). You should organize your writing to convey a central idea and use well-linked paragraphs to communicate that idea. Your story should have a strong beginning and an appropriate ending that ties the events of the story together.

a) Use an Organizer

You may find it helpful to use a writing organizer. Some examples are shown below.

Story Title				
Beginning	**Middle**	**End**	**Characters**	**Setting**

Story Web

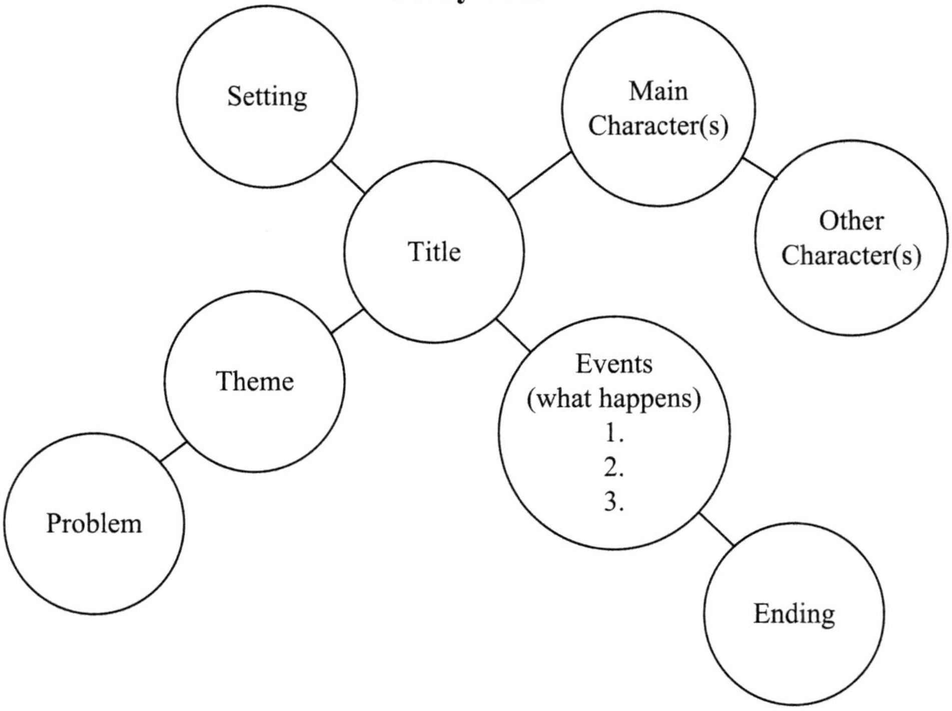

Story Planning Chart	
Title	
Setting	
Theme	
Problem	
Main Character(s)	
Other Character(s)	
Plot (Events/Action)	
Ending	

Story Outline

Title

Introductory Paragraph

- setting
- main character(s)

Second Paragraph

- problem
- other character(s)
- action/events

Other Paragraphs

- more action or events that add to the plot

Closing Paragraph

- how the problem is solved
- how the story ends

Choose the organizer that works best for you. Remember, you should spend about ten minutes planning your story **before** you actually begin writing it. These organizers help keep your planning orderly.

b) Sequence of Events—Plot

Careful plot development involves thinking about the order of the story's events before writing them. It is a good idea to stop writing occasionally and read what you have written. Does it make sense? Will the reader be able to follow what is happening? Are the events and the character reactions linked in a meaningful and engaging way?

If you are writing a mystery, you could consider surprising the reader. You might leave clues for the reader to find or you might have the story take an unexpected turn. If you are writing a story with a theme like friendship, you could describe the connections between characters and provide details about the relationships. What have the friends done together that has resulted in their current bond? Think about explaining what they like, what they have in common, or what they dream of.

c) Paragraphing

Paragraphs are groups of sentences separated into physical chunks on the page. While paragraphs can be identified by the blank spaces left between them, they are most easily identified by the indentation of their first sentence. There are many types of paragraphs, but two that are used in narrative writing are the narrative paragraph and the descriptive paragraph.

A **narrative paragraph** is a group of sentences telling about one idea or event. Each sentence in a narrative paragraph should tell about this main idea or event. We call the main idea or event the *topic*. The sentences within the paragraph should provide supporting details about the topic and follow a logical order. Generally, a narrative paragraph will have an interesting beginning sentence and a strong closing sentence.

A **descriptive paragraph** is a group of sentences describing a person, place, or thing. The opening sentence usually states what is being described (the topic). Each subsequent sentence in the paragraph should add more descriptive details about the topic. A descriptive paragraph should help the reader create a mental picture. Use adjectives, adverbs, strong verbs, and specific nouns to bring your story to life.

d) Coherence

Coherence refers to the way in which the story events and character actions "make sense" and lead to a meaningful ending. There are many ways to organize story events. Many stories begin with general or less important events and build up to a climax or turning point. Other stories may begin with a flashback in time and then return to the present action. You can choose how to organize the events of your story, but regardless of your choice, there should be connections between the events of the story that make sense and flow logically.

e) Time Frame

Closely related to the idea of coherence is the notion of time frame. A time frame is basically the "when" of your story. When does the story begin? What time of day? What time of year? How long does your story last? An afternoon, overnight, or over several years? As time passes, you need to link the events of the story together. Make sure that your story's time frame is in a meaningful order that engages the reader. Be sure to use words that give the reader clues to the time frame: yesterday, some time later, meanwhile, after supper, before, the next day, etc.

3. Sentence Structure

Using a variety of sentence structures creates interest in a story. Consider the following suggestions as you develop and edit your narrative.

• *Run-on Sentences*

When writing a narrative, be careful to avoid run-on sentences. Run-on sentences generally occur when two or more complete sentences are joined together without the proper punctuation. Though you want to use a variety of sentence types and lengths in your writing, be careful to avoid run-ons. A longer sentence is not necessarily a better one. Consider this example:

Bobby loves to draw cartoon strips he is a talented artist.

This is an incorrect sentence because the statements "Bobby loves to draw cartoon strips" and "he is a talented artist" can both stand alone as complete sentences. They are both independent clauses. They cannot run together into one sentence without somehow separating them. There are several ways to fix these types of sentences.

1. You could separate the two clauses into two sentences: *Bobby loves to draw cartoon strips. He is a talented artist.*
2. You could use a semicolon to properly punctuate the two clauses: *Bobby loves to draw cartoon strips; he is a talented artist.*
3. You could use a coordinating conjunction (and, but, or, for, yet, nor, so) to properly separate the two clauses: *Bobby is a talented artist and he loves to draw cartoon strips.*
4. You could use a subordinating conjunction (after, although, before, unless, as, because, even though, if, since, until, when, while) to properly separate the two clauses: *Since Bobby is a talented artist, he loves to draw cartoon strips.*
5. You could use a semicolon and transitional word or phrase (however, on the other hand, therefore, otherwise) to properly separate the two clauses: *Bobby is a talented artist; therefore, he loves to draw cartoon strips.*

- *Complete Versus Incomplete Sentences*

A sentence is a group of words that expresses a complete thought. The group of words should make sense by itself. Compare the following examples to determine which example provides a complete thought:

While Sonia was hurrying to the station.

Kevin finished the test early.

If you think that the second sentence expresses a complete thought, you are correct. A complete sentence has a subject and a predicate. The subject of a sentence tells *what* it is that you are talking about—the person, place, or thing. The predicate tells something *about* the subject. Every complete sentence must have a subject *and* a predicate.

In the second example, *Kevin* is the subject of the sentence, and *finished the test early* is the predicate. In the first example, however, we are left wondering what happened while Sonia was hurrying to the station. It is not a complete sentence because it is not a complete thought. While writing your story, make sure that you write in complete sentences. By maintaining solid sentence structure, you will be able to express your ideas more clearly.

- *Sentence Variety*

Sometimes a series of sentences that are grammatically correct is uninteresting because all the sentences in the series have the same length or pattern. You may want to consider using a variety of sentence structures and sentence types to make your writing more interesting. Writing should have short, medium, and long sentences. It should also include statements, questions, and exclamations.

One way to write interesting sentences is to **combine** sentences. Here are two examples.

Instead of saying: *Priya was tired. Alanna was tired.*

Combine the sentences to say: *Priya and Alanna were tired.*

Instead of saying: *We went to the mall. We ate lunch.*

Combine the sentences to say: *We went to the mall and ate lunch.*

Try using words like these to combine sentences in different ways:

later	after	while	although	when	however
as soon as	before	instead	just then	as	and

Instead of saying: *Shirley waited at the corner. Dan came running toward her.*

Combine the sentences to say: *Shirley waited at the corner while Dan came running toward her.*

Instead of saying: *Sam looked frightened. Sam continued to try his best.*

Combine the sentences to say: *Although Sam looked frightened, he continued to try his best.*

Another way to write interesting sentences is to **vary** how your sentences **begin**. Varying sentence beginnings can help your writing become more interesting and engaging. Read the following paragraphs to discover the difference that a variety of sentence beginnings can make.

> A moose stood in my backyard. The moose looked as if it stood there all the time. The moose didn't seem nervous or frightened. The moose didn't seem angered or about to charge. The moose didn't seem to notice me as I gazed out our back door. Then, the moose turned its head and stared right at me. Then, it took a few steps in my direction. Then, I froze. Then, I wondered if the moose might try to smash through our back door. Then, it simply turned away from me and headed back out to the forest.

Here is the same paragraph written with a variety of sentence beginnings.

> A moose stood in my backyard. It gazed around casually as if it stood there all the time. Sniffing and looking about, the moose didn't appear nervous or frightened at all. Although I knew that situations like this could be dangerous, the moose didn't seem angered or ready to charge. I wondered if the moose even noticed me as I looked out our back door. Suddenly, the moose turned its head and stared directly at me. My eyes widened as the moose took a few steps in my direction. I froze. Would the moose try to smash through our back door? Before I could react, the moose turned away from me and headed back out to the forest.

When writing a story, consider using some of these sentence starters to help you begin your sentences in a variety of ways.

Carefully,... Suddenly,... Happily,... Excitedly,... Thoughtfully,...
Without hesitation,...
Before I knew what had happened,...
My eyes widened...
Perhaps if I...
I wondered if...

4. Vocabulary

The most interesting stories are those that engage the reader. A story that has rich details about the setting and the character(s) enable the reader to "see" the story in his/her head. Details help the reader to understand how a character feels, thinks, or acts. Details can help a reader feel as though he or she is right inside the story.

Often, young writers are told to add more detail to their stories, but they do not have a clear sense of why their stories need elaborative detail. Think about the following vocabulary choices when you attempt to add elaborative detail.

- *Choose Strong Words*

Words that are vague or commonly used can often be replaced by more specific words that provide more detail. Consider this example:

My mom is a nice woman.

Though there is nothing wrong with this sentence, consider how much more specific the following sentence is:

My mom is a kind-hearted woman.

Can you think of more specific words to use in place of the bolded words in each of these sentences?

*Ryan **went** up the stairs and slammed his bedroom door.*

*The elephant **went** across the stream.*

Sometimes students are tempted to overuse a thesaurus when searching for interesting vocabulary choices. Be careful! Make sure that the word you choose as a replacement is **appropriate** to the context. You want to use interesting words, but you need to use them accurately. For example, if you wanted to change the word *plenty* in the sentence *We had plenty of food for the party*, it would not be appropriate to substitute the word *flood* for the word *plenty* even though *flood* is listed in the thesaurus as a synonym for *plenty*.

- *Show, Don't Tell*

Words like *very* and *really* are often overused and have little effect. Changing *the big house* to *the very big house* or to *the very, very big house* does not add descriptive detail. These word choices are repetitive and unconvincing.

Instead, try the **show, don't tell** technique. Try to take your reader into your story by describing how things look, sound, smell, taste, or feel.

Here is an example of **telling**:

> *The boy was rich. He lived in a really, really big house.*

This example does not provide details that help the reader to create a mental image of the house.

Here is an example of **showing**:

> *Stepping into his place for the first time, I could not believe that this enormous home could belong to just one family. The entrance alone provided enough room for a whole family to dine in.*

The second description draws the reader into the story by providing enough detail to create a mental picture of the size of the house. Words that describe give the reader a clearer picture of your thoughts and ultimately make your story more interesting to read.

Here is another example of **telling**: *I missed my bus this morning.*

Here is the same idea written as an example of **showing**: *Just as I turned the corner, I could see the bright yellow school bus pulling away from the curb.*

- *Avoid a List of Adjectives*

Using too many descriptive words together in a list can unnecessarily slow your story down. Here is an example of excessive adjective use:

The small, cute, fluffy, little, friendly kitten belonged to Sam.

You may find it more effective to describe Sam's kitten in more than one sentence or to develop the description throughout the story. For example, *The fluffy little kitten belonged to Sam. It was so small that Sam could carry it in his jacket pocket.*

- *Emphasize Important Details*

When adding detail to your story, it is important to decide where enhancing details should be included. Not every event and character needs to be described in equal detail. Decide which story events, objects, settings, or character actions are most important in your story. Create vivid images and specific details for these story elements. Consider this example:

I cooked supper.

Now, compare it with the following sentence:

Last night I cooked a pot of delicious chili because it was my mother's birthday.

Which sentence provides you with more information about the characters in the story? Which sentence would you use?

- *Figurative Language*

Figurative language adds interest to writing that is otherwise literal. A well-chosen figure of speech can add depth and meaning to ordinary descriptions. Some of the more commonly used figures of speech are simile, metaphor, and personification. A **simile** compares unlike objects or ideas using the words "like" or "as." For example, the statement *The tarmac was as hot as the Sahara Desert* offers a more vivid description of the hot temperature than the statement *The temperature on the tarmac was 35° Celsius.* A **metaphor** also compares unlike objects or ideas, but without using the prepositions "like" or "as." If Janet ran her race extremely fast, we could say, *She flew around the course on eagle's wings.* This metaphor compares Janet's speed with that of an eagle. **Personification** attributes human characteristics to animals and other objects.

For example, in the sentence *Our usual summer storms were mere complaints compared with the tornado that raged across our yard late that afternoon*, human qualities personify the wind. This helps the reader to sense the intensity of the wind.

Again, be careful not to overuse figurative language. Too many similes, for example, might ruin their effect.

5. Conventions

a) Mechanics

i) Punctuation

Using appropriate punctuation helps you to express your ideas clearly. A brief description of commonly used punctuation follows.

- *The Period*

A period is placed at the end of every sentence that is a statement. It is like a stop sign. The question you need to ask is, "When do I need to stop?" To figure out where one sentence ends and another begins, carefully read what you have written. Look for a place where one idea or thought ends and another begins. If, while you read over your work, you naturally stop at a certain point, it is likely that is where the complete idea is concluded and a period or some other form of punctuation is needed.

- *The Question Mark*

Sentences that begin with words such as *when*, *where*, *why*, *how*, *who*, *is*, *are*, and *which* are usually questions. A question requires an answer of some sort. Questioning statements end with a question mark rather than a period. Look at the following examples:

When the lights went out, we became frightened.

Since no response is required, the statement ends in a period.

When did the lights go out?

This time a response is required, so the statement ends in a question mark.

- *The Exclamation Mark*

The exclamation mark is used to show expression and often appears at the end of a command. For example, you may use an exclamation mark in the following sentences:

Wow! Stop! Oh no! I could not believe my eyes!

- *The Comma*

The comma helps clarify meaning in writing. It sets apart certain ideas in sentences, indicating the relationship of one clause to the next. Consider the following examples:

Mrs. Jones our teacher unfortunately broke her leg.

While we were eating the dog began to whimper.

On the path leading to the basement steps were heard.

None of these sentences contains commas. You can see how difficult it is to read these sentences when there are no commas to organize the phrases within the sentences. Now, read the same sentences with commas.

Mrs. Jones, our teacher, unfortunately broke her leg.

While we were eating, the dog began to whimper.

On the path leading to the basement, steps were heard.

Immediately, the meaning of each sentence becomes clear. You should also recognize that it is important not to use the comma too often because commas have the effect of slowing down the reader. Too many commas can break up the flow of your writing and make it more difficult for your reader to follow.

The comma is also used to separate quoted speech from other language in writing. Read the following sentence:

His mother said, "Don't accuse me of stealing. I did not go anywhere near that store."

In examples of this type, the comma immediately follows the last word before the first set of quotation marks.

"Don't accuse me of stealing. I did not go anywhere near that store," his mother said.

In examples of this type, the comma immediately follows the last quoted word. It is important to remember that the comma falls inside the quotation mark, not outside it.

- *The Colon*

The colon directs the reader's attention to the phrase or clause that follows it. The colon serves three primary purposes:

1. It connects two independent clauses when the second one explains or illustrates the first.

    When I flew to London for my holiday, I realized two things: driving on the wrong side of the road causes accidents and disliking tea is considered strange.
    The striking baseball players wanted just one thing: clean uniforms.

2. It introduces a list described in the first clause.

    The city of New York offers the following attractions for first-time visitors: a dazzling nightlife, famous landmarks, and cabbies aspiring to be comedians.

3. It introduces a long quotation.

- *The Apostrophe*

Apostrophes are often confusing because they can be used in two different ways: as a contraction and to show possession.

An example of how an apostrophe is used in a contraction is the word "don't." The words "do" and "not" have been contracted, or shortened, to form the word "don't."

An example of how an apostrophe is used to show possession is the word "sister's." The apostrophe followed by the letter "s" indicates that something belongs to the sister. For example, instead of saying *The dog that belonged to her sister*, you can say *Her sister's dog*.

An exception to this explanation involves the word "it." Although an apostrophe followed by "s" indicates possession when used with a proper noun (Jane's hockey stick, Bob's hair gel), following "it" with an apostrophe and "s" indicates the contraction of "it is." To indicate possession using the pronoun "it," simply add the "s" without an apostrophe. For example, in this statement about a building, *Its colour has faded over time*, "its" refers to the attribute (colour) that is possessed by the building. In the sentence *It's now coloured a faded red*, the contraction has been used. To decide if it is the contraction or the possessive form of "it" that you should use, try seeing if the sentence still makes sense when you substitute "it is" for "it's." The sentence *It's now coloured a faded red* still makes sense when you substitute "it is."

- *Quotation Marks*

A quotation is something that someone has said. It is the exact words spoken (or written) by that person. For example,

> *"To be or not to be, that is the question," is from a play by Shakespeare.*

Notice that you set apart what is said by using quotation marks (" "). Quotation marks are used to mark the start and the end of a quotation and always come in pairs. You will probably most often use quotations in your narrative writing to indicate dialogue in conversations.

Remember that a comma should be used to separate the quotation from the rest of the sentence. If the quotation is at the start of a sentence, the comma needs to be placed inside the second set of quotation marks. For example,

> *"It is time to get going," suggested Roger.*

If the quotation is at the end of a sentence, the comma belongs in front of the first set of quotation marks. For example,

> *Roger suggested, "It is time to get going."*

In both of these situations, the quotation begins with a capital letter.

Sometimes, you may want to divide a quotation into two parts, as in the following example:

> *"Come to the grocery store," suggested Mike, "and help me choose Mom's birthday cake."*

When you divide a quotation, two sets of quotation marks are necessary. Notice where the commas are placed. When you use a divided quotation, you only capitalize the beginning of the quotation; the second part is not capitalized.

When writing dialogue, remember to begin a new paragraph every time there is a new speaker.

Quotation marks are also used around titles of shorter pieces of text such as episodes from television shows, essays within larger works, poems, and short stories. For example,

> *Elton John sang "Goodbye England's Rose" at Princess Diana's funeral.*

> *My favourite poem is William Shakespeare's sonnet "Let Me Not to the Marriage of True Minds."*

• *Parentheses*

When you want to add information to a sentence to help the reader better understand your ideas, you can use parentheses. No commas are needed when parentheses are used. For example,

Five years later, Billy Jax (the well-known whiz kid) won the contest.

• *Ellipses*

Ellipses are a series of three dots with spaces between them. You can use ellipses to show that words of a sentence have been left out. Ellipses can also be used to indicate dramatic pauses in speech, thoughts, or action. For example,

The weatherman stated, "Heavy rain, winds, and snow are expected . . . until the end of the week."
I just wanted to . . . hear my name.

ii) Capitalization

Although there are many special rules for capitalization, the following four rules are the most applicable to writing a narrative:

1. Capitalize the first words of sentences, including sentences used in quotations.

2. Capitalize proper nouns, including any specific person, place, or thing. For instance, capitalize *Suzie Walker*, *Happyville School*, *Edmonton*, *December*, *Christmas Day*, *Doctor Newman*, and *Artemis Fowl*. However, do not capitalize common nouns such as *the girl*, *a school*, *our city*, *a month*, *the day*, *the doctor*, or *a book*.

3. Always capitalize the word "I."

4. Capitalize some abbreviations and acronyms. For example, R.S.V.P., an abbreviation for a French phrase that means "please respond," and Ave., an abbreviation for Avenue, both require capital letters.

Capitalization can also be useful when you are trying to emphasize a certain word or create an emotional response. For example,

WOW! I could not believe my eyes. My brother was flying!

iii) Spelling

The importance of correct spelling needs to be emphasized. Spelling mistakes may indicate to your reader that you have been careless about the piece that you have written. Use a dictionary and/or a thesaurus whenever you write. Take advantage of these tools and try to give yourself enough time to slowly read through your work.

b) Usage

i) Verb Tense

The tense of a verb tells the reader when the action happens. The most common verb tenses you will use in your writing are the past tense (before), the present tense (now), and the future tense (later).

Here is an example of the three tenses of the verb *to work.*

Past tense	Present tense	Future tense
He worked.	*He works.*	*He will work.*

When you plan a story, you should think about when your story will take place: the past, the present, the future, or some combination of these time frames. You may decide to begin your story in the present but include flashback sequences. Make sure that when you are writing in the present, your verbs reflect the present tense. When you use a flashback sequence, make sure that the verbs are written in the past tense. Whatever you decide, make sure that you use consistent verb tenses in your narrative writing.

ii) Subject–Verb Agreement

The verb that you use in a sentence must agree with your subject in *number* and in *person.* So, if your subject is singular (one subject), your verb must also be singular; however, if your subject is plural (more than one subject), then your verb must be plural. If your subject is in the first person (I), your verb must agree with "I." If your subject is in the second (you) or third (he, she) person, your verb must agree with the relevant pronoun. For example,

Incorrect: *For years,* ***scientists has been*** *talking about the effects of global warming.*

Correct: *For years,* ***scientists have been*** *talking about the effects of global warming.*

In the first example, the subject is plural, but the verb is singular. To correct this, the verb needs to be changed to the plural form.

iii) Pronouns

Pronouns are words that take the place of nouns in referring to a person, place, thing, or idea. Using pronouns effectively allows you to avoid writing in a manner that may seem confusing and overly repetitive.

Read the following sentences and note the difference that the pronouns make.

Without pronouns: *Chamberlain and Chamberlain's team raced to win, but Chamberlain and Chamberlain's team weren't fast enough today.*

With pronouns: *Chamberlain and his team raced to win, but they weren't fast enough today.*

The second sentence, which uses pronouns, is a much smoother sentence and is therefore much easier to read and understand. Some common pronouns are *I*, *my*, *me*, *mine*, *we*, *our*, *us*, *you*, *your*, *he*, *him*, *his*, *she*, *her*, *they*, *them*, *their*, *it*, *herself*, *yourself*, and *each other*.

iv) Pronoun–Antecedent Agreement

A pronoun must agree in gender (masculine or feminine) and number (singular or plural) with its antecedent (the noun that the pronoun refers to). For example,

Incorrect: *A **candidate** for school council must be recommended by **their** teacher.*

Correct: *A **candidate** for school council must be recommended by **her** teacher.*

Correct: *A **candidate** for school council must be recommended by **his** teacher.*

Correct: ***Candidates** for school council must be recommended by **their** teacher.*

v) Comparative and Superlative Forms of Adjectives and Adverbs

Comparatives and superlatives are special forms of adjectives and adverbs. They are used to compare things. When we compare *two things*, we use the comparative form. For example,

> *A car is much **more expensive** than a lollipop.*
>
> *Five plus five is **greater** than four plus four.*

When we compare *more than two things*, we use the superlative form. For example,

*That was the **best** movie I have ever seen.*

*I wanted to buy the **largest** dog in the window.*

The chart below provides some examples that compare the base form of an adjective or adverb with the comparative and superlatives forms of the same word.

Base	Comparative	Superlative
fast	*faster*	*fastest*
good	*better*	*best*
wide	*wider*	*widest*
bad	*worse*	*worst*
quickly	*more quickly*	*most quickly*
harmful	*more harmful*	*most harmful*

vi) Subordinate Clauses and Coordinate Conjunctions

A clause is a group of words containing a subject and a predicate. A subordinate clause is a group of words that cannot stand alone as a sentence. Using subordinate clauses allows you to create interesting sentences by combining ideas. For example,

*My sister, **who is a doctor**, has four children.*
***While I clean my room**, I like to listen to music.*

The clauses *who is a doctor* and *while I clean my room* cannot stand alone as sentences and are therefore called subordinate clauses. Subordinate clauses add information to a sentence but are not complete ideas on their own.

Coordinating conjunctions are words used to join two clauses together. Some examples of coordinating conjunctions are *for*, *and*, *not*, *but*, *or*, *yet*, and *so*. These simple words can be used to join ideas and create complex sentences. For example,

*Wendy loved to read books **but** did not enjoy magazines.*
*John heard the weather report **and** hurried home.*
*The sun was shining brightly, **yet** the air was still cold.*

6. A Summary of Important Narrative Writing Elements

The narrative writing assignment allows you to be as imaginative as possible. The following reminders may help you to write your narrative clearly and effectively.

Content

- Plan your story and the events you will write about before you begin.
- Choose one storyline and stay on topic.
- Make sure that every event relates to your storyline.
- Choose a genre (mystery, adventure, drama, etc.) and stick to it.
- Use descriptive details to enhance your story events.
- Tell your story in an interesting way.
- Develop a story voice (funny, sarcastic, serious, poetic, gripping, etc.)

Organization

- Order the events of your story before you write.
- Begin your story by introducing the characters and the storyline in an interesting way.
- Describe what characters are thinking and how they are acting.
- Explain how one event leads to another.
- Break your writing into paragraphs.
- Build relationships between actions and characters.
- Tie everything together in the end.
- Work to create a reader response. Try to leave the reader smiling, crying, intrigued, etc.

Sentence Structure

- Write in complete sentences.
- Avoid run-on sentences.
- Vary sentence beginnings.
- Vary sentence type.
- Vary sentence length.

Vocabulary

- Describe events, characters, and settings accurately and effectively.
- Try to describe the incident you are imagining as clearly as possible.
- Use details to create a visual picture in the reader's mind.
- Use descriptive adjectives, adverbs, and figures of speech to add interest and detail to your writing.

Conventions

- Begin all sentences with capital letters.
- End all sentences with periods, exclamation marks, or question marks.
- Enclose conversation in quotation marks.
- Check unknown spellings in a dictionary.
- Check for subject–verb and pronoun–antecedent agreement.

A Final Note on Your Narrative

When you have completed your first draft, take time to reread your work. Consider the following checklist:

- ❑ Does every sentence make sense?
- ❑ Did I vary the length and type of sentences?
- ❑ Have I used capital letters correctly?
- ❑ Have I given my story a title?
- ❑ Have I punctuated every sentence properly?
- ❑ Have I indented my paragraphs?
- ❑ Did I spell words correctly and check those I was unsure about?
- ❑ Did I make interesting vocabulary choices?
- ❑ Did I use words correctly?
- ❑ Do I have a beginning, middle, and end?
- ❑ Did I clearly say what I wanted to say?
- ❑ Did I stay on topic?

SECTION II — FUNCTIONAL WRITING

The functional writing section requires you to write a news article for a specific audience and to fulfill a specified purpose within a given context (situation). You should take about 40 minutes to complete Section II. Here is an example of a functional writing task from a previous exam.

The Situation

Your name is Kelly Brown. You are a writer for your school's newspaper. Recently, a teacher led a group of students and parents on a school trip to the Royal Tyrrell Museum in Drumheller. You interviewed some of the students, one of the parents, and the teacher. They told you why they went to the museum and talked about some of the interesting things they did on the trip. You have also visited the Royal Tyrrell Museum web site to gather additional information.

Assignment

Write a news article that will inform the readers about the purpose of the school trip to the Royal Tyrrell Museum and tell about some of the interesting things that the students did while they were in Drumheller on the trip.

Use the information provided on the next page to assist you as you write your news article.

Notes About the School Trip to the Royal Tyrrell Museum

Where did the group go? —Royal Tyrrell Museum —badlands surrounding Drumheller **Why did the group go?** —to explore the museum —to learn about dinosaurs —to learn about what paleontologists do **What happened?** —students participated in a fossil excavation —students worked with museum staff to uncover fossils at a dig site —students learned how to map and collect fossils —students participated in a "Behind-the-Scenes Tour" of the museum —students were able to explore all of the displays at the museum **Who was involved?** —students, teacher, parents —museum staff	**How did the group travel?** —school bus to Drumheller **Highlights of the trip** —sleeping in the Great Hall of the Dinosaurs —making plaster casts of excavated fossils —using tools to measure and identify fossils —hiking through the badlands —playing a variety of dinosaur games **How can people find out more information about the Royal Tyrrell Museum?** —through the web site www.tyrrellmuseum.com

You do not have to use all the information provided on this page.

You may include additional appropriate information in your writing.

When writing your news article, be sure to:

a) provide readers with **information** that will support the purpose of the news article

b) use a **style of writing** appropriate for a news article

c) use a **style of writing** appropriate for the audience

HOW THE FUNCTIONAL WRITING WILL BE GRADED

1. **Content:** Students effectively develop an appropriate response that incorporates significant information and appropriate details. Consideration is given to audience and purpose.

2. **Content Management:** Students communicate clearly by adhering to appropriate sentence structure, usage, mechanics, and format. Students use specific words and expressions accurately and effectively to communicate to the audience and to achieve their purpose. The number of errors in the story will be considered in relation to the length and complexity of the response.

Content and content management are equally weighted.

You will be given a topic to write about. Your article must be related to the topic. Those assignments that are off topic will be given a mark of "insufficient."

WRITING A NEWS ARTICLE

When you think about where you find news articles, you probably think about the news that you read in newspapers and magazines, hear on the radio, and see on television. However, you also hear or report "news" when you talk to your friends, parents, siblings, teachers, or others. You can improve your ability to write a good news article by studying the characteristics of news articles and reading, viewing, or listening to well-written news items.

There are three main functions of news articles: to inform, to entertain, and to persuade. Typically, your assignment will require that you write a news article that is designed to be informative. However, there may also be situations where incorporating elements of entertainment or persuasion is also appropriate. Your news article should contain objective, factual information, and be written in the third person (he, she, it, they). Your writing should be simple, clear, and to the point.

1. The Structure of a News Article

A news article usually consists of a headline, a byline, a dateline, and a body. Writing a news article is very different from writing a narrative. Generally, a narrative will build up to the climax, or most important part, of the story. The news article, on the other hand, begins with the most important information and then proceeds to less important information, leaving the least important to the end. The structure of a news article can be compared with an inverted pyramid. A news article begins with a lead paragraph that contains the most significant information in the story and then continues through the middle paragraphs to the concluding paragraph of the article. The following information gives you an overview of each part of a news article.

a) The Headline

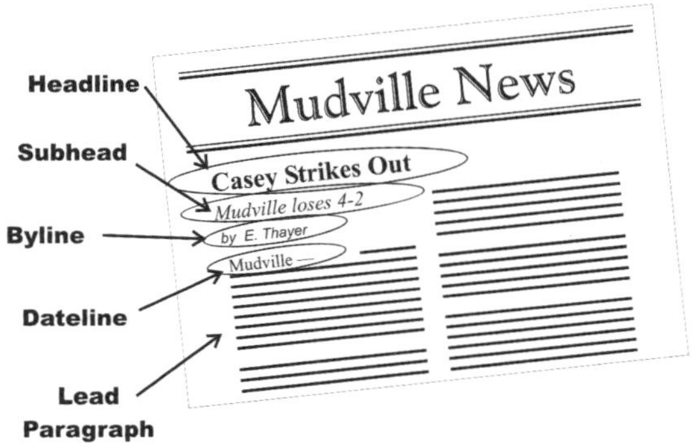

The headline is the title of your news article. It is a very brief summary of your news article. The headline must grab the reader's attention by using exciting and vivid words. It often contains a noun and a verb. All important words are capitalized and there is no punctuation at the end of the title.

b) The Subhead

Sometimes a subhead, or secondary title, appears immediately after the headline. A subhead provides additional information about the story. You do not have to include a subhead; it is optional.

c) The Byline

The byline is positioned after the subhead. As the name suggests, it is the **line** that tells who the story is **by**, that is, who wrote the article. You will be provided with a pseudonym (an imaginary name) for your news article. Use this name; **do not** use your own name.

d) The Dateline

The dateline usually appears at the beginning of an article; it is included at the start of the lead paragraph. It tells the reader where the story happened. It does not tell the date.

e) The Lead Paragraph

The beginning of a news article is called the lead, and it sets the structure for the rest of the article. The most important ideas of the article are included in the lead. A good lead usually answers the following questions: Who? What? When? Where? Why? and How? (the 5 Ws and How).

Who	the subject of the article. The article could be about a person, place, idea, event or object—basically anything about which an article can be written.
What	the action of the article. What has happened or what is currently happening.
When	the time frame of the article. Did the action take place last night, last week, or over the course of a month?
Where	the place the action is happening.
Why	explains the "what," or the action, of the article.
How	describes the sequence of events or actions that occurred.

The 5 Ws and How are usually covered in the first one or two sentences. The rest of the first paragraph may include additional details or important information

The first sentence of your lead, in particular, is very important. It must hook readers, and encourage them to continue reading. In most news articles, the first sentence gives answers to as many of the 5 Ws and How as possible, in as few words as possible. The first sentence should provide a good lead-in to the rest of the paragraph and article. The following is an example of a first sentence:

WHO	WHAT	WHERE	WHEN	WHY
"Thousands of students	*marched*	*in the streets of Ottawa*	*today*	*to protest violence in schools."*

Try to create an original and captivating lead. You might consider introducing your topic using a lead that:

- asks questions
- includes surprises
- creates suspense
- uses a quotation
- provokes a thought or idea
- describes who, what, or where

Think of a topic for a news article and try to develop a variety of leads. For example, what leads could you write about the circus coming to town?

f) The Middle Paragraphs

The middle paragraphs of a news article provide the reader with more details about the topic. There should be smooth transitions from one paragraph to the next to keep your article coherent. Remember to be *objective*—do not state your own opinion. The purpose of your article is to convey **facts**. You may include quotations from people involved in the story, and these quotations can express *their opinions*. Make sure that you properly identify who is speaking. If the speaker has a title or a specific role in the event, you may want to draw attention to it. For example:

> *"The kids wear clothes that look just like ours," Tara Clarke, a participant in the exchange, commented.*
>
> *"We have just invested a great deal of resources into this programme," said Norma Jacob, Minister of Education.*

If you have already referred to the speaker at some point in your article, you may subsequently refer to the speaker by their last name only. For example:

> *"As much as I enjoyed the trip, I am happy to be home," Clarke stated.*

In this example, we used *Clarke* instead of *Tara Clarke* as we had already explained who she was earlier in the article.

Remember, you may say what other people think, but you must clearly indicate to whom the thoughts or ideas belong. You can also use information supplied in the prompt to determine what a person involved in the event might say. For example, if the prompt supplies you with information about a lost animal's habits, you could report this information through an official. For example:

> *"I can't believe that our cougar is gone! If you see her, do not approach her. Call the police immediately. She is likely frightened and this may cause her to attack," Terry Seth, the head zookeeper at Happy Ville, remarked.*

g) The Last Paragraph

The last paragraph concludes and summarizes the article. It may also provide a call-to-action—a suggestion of what readers can do in response to the article. For example, the last paragraph of an article about an earthquake could include information about where readers could donate money, clothes, or blankets to help those affected. If the article was about a lost cougar, you might provide a phone number that people could call should they spot the lost animal. Here are a couple of writing tips for your final paragraph:

- Do not use phrases such as "*In summary*" or "*To conclude*". These are ordinary and overused phrases. Furthermore, they do not fit the tone of an objective news article.
- Do not leave the reader hanging. Bring closure to your article.

2. Organizing Your News Article

You should spend about 10 minutes planning before you begin writing. Examples of organizational tools that you may wish to use when planning your article are given below.

TOOL 1: RAFTS Model

R...Role	Example:	R...Role	Student reporter
A...Audience		A...Audience	Parents, teachers, students
F...Format		F...Format	News article
T...Topic		T...Topic	Cougar has escaped
S...Strong Verb		S...Strong Verb	To inform

TOOL 2:

Topic:

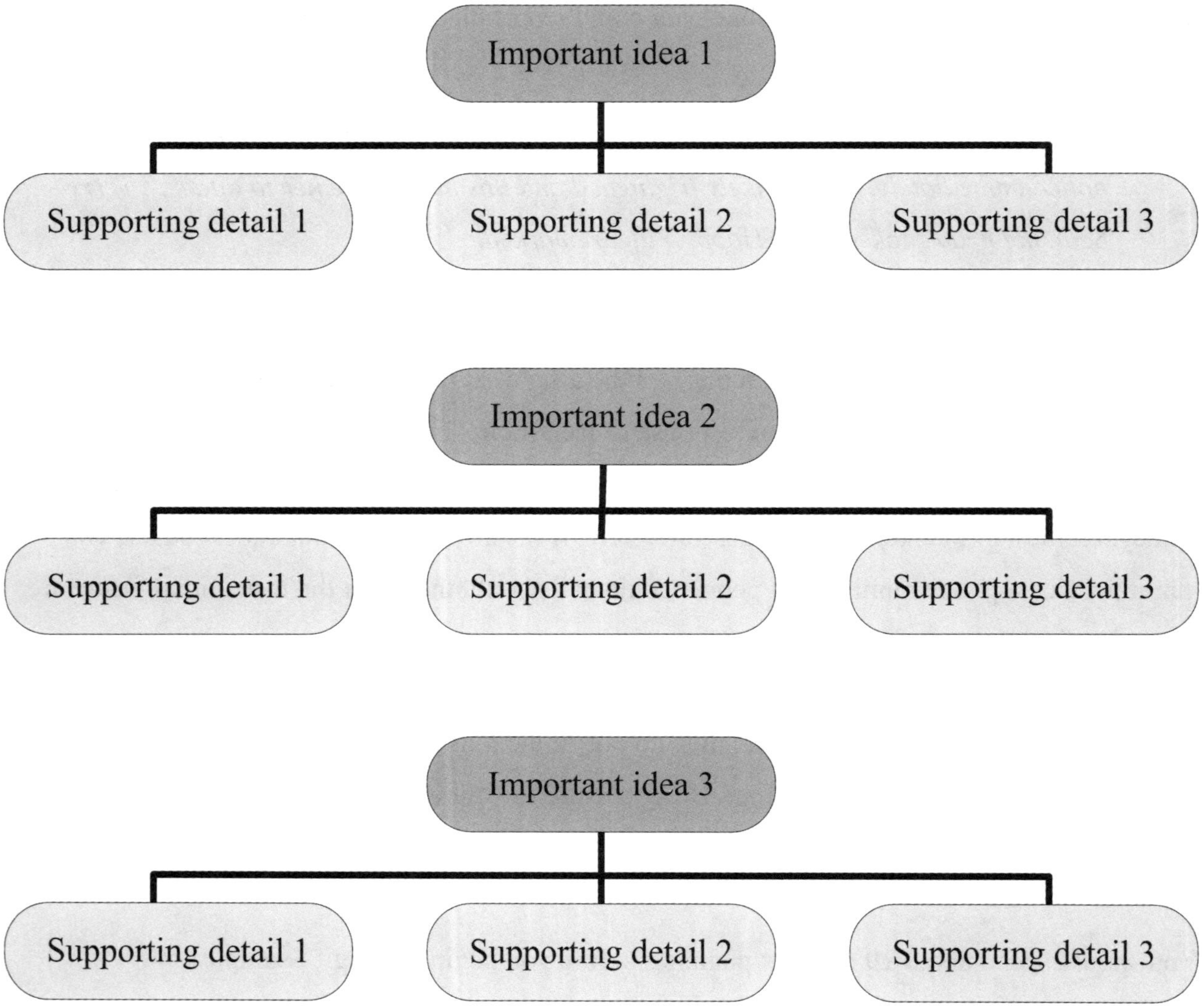
Important idea 1
Supporting detail 1
Supporting detail 2
Supporting detail 3
Important idea 2
Supporting detail 1
Supporting detail 2
Supporting detail 3
Important idea 3
Supporting detail 1
Supporting detail 2
Supporting detail 3

TOOL 3:

Topic:

Headline:

Byline:

Lead:

TOOL 4:

Quotes:

Who?

What?

Where?

When?

Why?

How?

3. Accuracy and Effectiveness of Words and Expressions

Since you are writing a news article, not a narrative, try to maintain a factual tone; resist the temptation to "tell a story." The words that you choose can dramatically impact the tone of your article, so try to choose words and expressions that are clear, concise, and to the point. Consider these examples:

noted	joined	explained	commented	added
thrilled	surprised	shocked	this event	impacted
sudden and devastating change		remarkable achievement		horrified to discover

You should also maintain an active voice in your writing. In the active voice, the subject of the sentence is the performer of the action and the object is the receiver of the action. In comparison, in the passive voice, the subject of the sentence is the receiver of the action. For example:

Active voice: *Julia Hewitt* ***presented*** *the first award of the evening.*

Passive voice: *The first award of the evening* ***was presented*** *by Julia Hewitt.*

4. Sentence Structure, Mechanics, and Usage

The same suggestions as described in Section I for sentence structure, mechanics, and usage apply to the news article. Review those pages for specific suggestions.

A Summary of Important Functional Writing Elements

Headline

- *Tells what the article is about*
- *Is brief but catchy*

Lead Paragraph—Essential Information

- *Includes the 5Ws and How*
- *Uses a lead that grabs the reader's attention*
- *Uses an appropriate tone for a news article*

Middle Paragraphs—Additional Information

- *Further describes the event*
- *Includes at least one quotation from someone involved in the event and properly identifies the speaker*
- *Includes smooth transitions from one paragraph to the next*

Last Paragraph—Conclusion

- *Summarizes what has been said*
- *May include advice or a call-to-action*
- *Ends in an interesting manner*

Organization

- *Article begins with important ideas*
- *Supporting details come later*
- *Paragraphs are concise and clear*
- *Events are logically ordered throughout*

Words and Expressions

- *Uses vocabulary that is clear, concise, and to the point*
- *Uses an active voice*
- *Uses descriptive words*

Sentence Structure, Mechanics, and Usage

- *Uses correct and varied sentence structure, spelling, capitalization and punctuation*
- *Uses quotation marks around a speaker's comments*
- *Uses a consistent verb tense*
- *Ensures subject–verb and pronoun–antecedent agreement*

A Final Note on Your News Article

When you have completed your first draft, take time to reread your work. Ask yourself the following questions.

- ❑ Is my purpose for writing clear?
- ❑ Does my opening encourage the reader to want to know more?
- ❑ Have I provided enough information?
- ❑ Have I provided details to explain my purpose?
- ❑ Have I considered my audience by using an appropriate tone?
- ❑ Have I used accurate and effective words and expressions?
- ❑ Have I used the correct format for my purpose?
- ❑ Have I used proper sentence structure, grammar, spelling, and punctuation?

READING

Part B: Reading

The reading section of the Grade 6 English Language Arts Provincial Achievement Test requires you to answer 50 multiple-choice questions based on various reading selections. These reading selections generally include fictional passages, informational texts, poetry, and cartoon strips. You will be given 60 minutes to complete this section, with an additional 30 minutes to be provided if needed.

Answering reading comprehension questions involves the following three steps.

- **Interpreting the information:** deciding what information is required by the question.
- **Locating the required information:** finding information that is "right there" in the text; or, when the answer is not in the text, inferring it based on what is in the text.
- **Formulating an appropriate answer:** in a multiple-choice test, choosing the appropriate answer from one of the alternatives (A, B, C, or D).

APPROACHING THE TEXT

There are two common approaches to answering multiple-choice reading comprehension questions.

1. Read the entire selection, thinking about the meaning of the selection as you read. Once you have read the entire selection, read the first question and the alternatives. Check the reading passage for evidence that supports one of the alternatives. Complete each question in the same manner, carefully checking the text for evidence that supports one of the alternatives.

2. Read all of the questions about the reading selection first. Then, read the entire passage to find the answers to the questions.

Both of these approaches are effective. Consider trying out both techniques and deciding which one works best for you.

UNDERSTANDING THE TEXT

There are many levels at which we understand texts, ranging from very simple to very complex. Generally, we can group our understanding of texts into four levels of comprehension. Below is a short reading passage followed by an explanation of how it would be understood at each of the four levels of comprehension.

> *Sally returned home after searching the streets for hours. She sat down on her front steps and began to cry. In her hand, she held a leash with the name "Snoopy" embossed on the leather handle.*

1. **Literal comprehension** is an understanding of information that is clearly stated in the text. For example:

   What is the name of the girl in the story? (Sally)

   When Sally sat down, what happened? (She began to cry)

   What was Sally holding? (A leash)

   When answering literal comprehension questions, the best strategy is to reread the text and simply find the answer.

2. **Inferential comprehension** is an understanding of the implied message of the text. These types of questions ask you for information that is suggested by the text but never directly stated. For example:

   How is Sally feeling? (Sad)

   When answering inferential comprehension questions, look for clues within the text that imply, or suggest, meaning. In this example, nowhere in the text does it actually state that Sally is sad; however, a strong clue as to how Sally may be feeling is the fact that she has begun to cry.

3. **Applied comprehension** is an understanding that requires the reader to move beyond the text and draw on his or her own previous knowledge. In these types of questions, you need to combine the stated and implied information and apply it to what you already know. For example:

    Who is Snoopy? (A dog, a cat, another pet)

    When answering applied comprehension questions, compare the stated and implied information within the text to your own knowledge to arrive at a logical conclusion. In this example, the stated information (the name Snoopy is embossed on a leash), the implied information (Sally cares about Snoopy), and your own knowledge (leashes are used for walking pets) are all required to correctly answer the question.

4. **Judgement comprehension** is an understanding that requires the reader to make a judgement that can be supported by the reading selection. For example:

    What else might Sally do to find her pet?

    There may be several acceptable answers to this question, but the "best" answer in a multiple-choice test will be supported by the facts of the story. These types of questions will often include words like **best**, **most clearly**, or **most strongly** in the question stem.

READING COMPREHENSION STRATEGIES

Reading comprehension strategies are tools that you can use to help you to make sense of what you read. This section is designed to provide you with some specific reading strategies that good readers use to make sure that they understand what they read. The following explanations and examples will show you how to use these strategies when you read prose, poetry, and visual texts.

Strategy 1—Using Prior Knowledge

Using prior knowledge means building on your own background knowledge (previous understanding and experiences) to help you understand the text you are reading. Readers usually comprehend a text better when they think actively about it and apply their background knowledge to it.

To apply this strategy, try to make connections between what you know and what you are reading. Try asking yourself the following questions as your read.

- ❑ What does this story remind me of?
- ❑ What do I already know about the topic I am reading about?
- ❑ Does this story remind me of any other stories I have read before?
- ❑ Is there something in this text that is like something I already know?

Strategy 2—Predicting

This strategy requires you to predict what you will learn or what will happen in the text. Using your background knowledge and clues from the text, you can form hypotheses (good guesses or predictions) as you read. You should be able to support your predictions with facts from the text.

To practice this strategy, try the following suggestions:

- ❑ Before you read,
    - ask "I wonder…" questions before you begin to read.
    - make predictions about the story; for example, "I think this story will be about…"
    - try to guess what the story might be about based on its title.
- ❑ As you read, stop and predict what might happen next.
- ❑ After you read, ask yourself if your predictions match the text. If not, why not?

Strategy 3—Monitoring for Meaning

This strategy involves continually checking your understanding of the material that you are reading. Using an inner voice, think about whether or not the text makes sense to you. Think about the broader (larger) meaning of the story.

To practice this strategy, try the following suggestions:

- Ask yourself regularly, "Do I understand what I just read?"
- As you read, think about what is happening in the story.
- Think about how the important ideas and details relate to each other.
- As you read, ask yourself questions about the story: who? when? what? where? why?
- After reading, think about any questions you still have.

Strategy 4—Visualizing: Go to the Movies in Your Head

Writers communicate information with words. As you read, you can use these words to create pictures in your mind of what is happening in the text. These images may include sights, sounds, and other sensory information. Visualizing like this can help you to remember information more easily than by words alone, and it can deepen your understanding of the text. Through visualization, you can create images of the characters, settings, and events of a story.

To practice visualizing while reading, try the following:

- Pause frequently and describe any pictures in your mind.
- After reading a passage, draw a picture of what you see in your mind.
- Work backward: look at wordless picture books and tell a story to match the pictures.

Strategy 5—Inferring

You can make inferences about the text that you are reading by combining your background knowledge and the information in the text to create meaning beyond what is directly stated in the text. Inferences may include conclusions, predictions, and new ideas. You can think of making inferences as being like imagining what is probably true.

To practice inferring while reading, ask yourself the following questions:

- ❑ Why did I think that would happen?
- ❑ What do I think this story is about?
- ❑ How do I think the character feels?
- ❑ How did I know that?
- ❑ What does the writer actually say?
- ❑ What does the writer lead me to believe?

Strategy 6—Determining Importance

This strategy is particularly useful for non-fiction and informational texts. The idea behind this strategy is to distinguish between the "must know" information and the less important details in a text. By identifying important ideas and themes, you can set aside less important ideas and pieces of information.

To practice determining importance while reading, try the following:

- ❑ Before reading, think about what you know about the topic and what you would like to learn.
- ❑ While reading, look for clues in the format of the text that might indicate importance. Pay attention to the first and last lines of a paragraph; the title; any headings or subheadings; captions; framed text (text with a box drawn around it); quotation marks; font size; font style (underlined text, italics, bolded text).
- ❑ Pay particular attention to pictures, illustrations, charts, and diagrams; they may provide you with important information.
- ❑ As you read, intend to remember.
- ❑ After reading, think about what the most important information you learned was.

Strategy 7—Synthesizing

Synthesizing is the ability to put elements together to form a whole. We can compare synthesis to the process of making a cake: we combine the cake mix, oil, eggs, and water, and then bake it to create a whole new thing—a cake. Synthesizing allows you to sort through the information in the text to make sense of it, and, in some cases, to act upon it.

To practice synthesizing, ask yourself the following questions:

- What was the author's purpose in writing this piece?
- What was the main idea of this story?
- What clues helped me to determine the main idea?
- How do different parts of this story connect with one another?
- Has my thinking changed after reading this piece?
- Can I think of a new title for this piece?

Strategy 8—Figure-it-out

If you encounter a comprehension problem when you are reading, you need to have different strategies to draw on to solve the problem you have encountered. There are a variety of "figure-it-out" strategies that you can use when you do not understand something you have read.

Here is a list of strategies to consider.

- Reread: if you can't make a picture in your mind or if you don't understand what you have just read, try reading it again. Sometimes a second reading is all that it takes!
- Skip ahead: sometimes you need to move on. If you don't understand something you have just read, skip ahead and continue reading. There may be information later on that helps you to understand the section that you are having trouble with. You can always go back and reread the difficult section later.
- Context clues: use the familiar words surrounding an unfamiliar word to help you determine the new word's meaning.
- Picture clues: use information from pictures to help make sense of what you have read.
- Ask for help: ask a teacher, parent, classmate, or sibling for help when you have tried your own strategies but still do not understand.

USING YOUR STRATEGIES WITH PROSE

Sometimes questions based on a specific text will require you to use only one of the strategies outlined previously. Other times, you will need to use more than one strategy. The following sample reading selections and reading comprehension questions provide you with the opportunity to practice both types of questions. Each question is followed by suggestions for applying the strategies. Before you read the suggestions, take a few minutes to generate your own response to each of the questions.

EXAMPLE 1

Read the following selection from *Natural Wonders of the World: Mount Everest.*

BECAUSE IT IS THERE

Until 1953, no human had ever stood atop the peak of Mount Everest. In fact, since neither Nepal nor Tibet welcomed outsiders before the turn of the 20th century, no Westerner had even come within 100 kilometres of Mount Everest's foothills until 1913. Cloaked in snow and ice, the mountain was considered sacred by local people. Tibetans called the soaring peak *Chomolungma*, "Goddess Mother of the World." The Nepalese called it *Sagarmatha,* "Forehead of the Sky." In 1921, a British reconnaissance team finally received permission from Tibet to explore Everest's North and East Faces. The team failed to summit (reach the peak) that year and the next, but one team member, George Leigh Mallory, decided to make a third attempt in 1924. When asked why he wanted to climb Mount Everest, Mallory replied, "Because it is there." On the morning of June 8, 1924, Mallory and partner Andrew Irvine set out for the summit from their camp at 8,138 metres. Hours later, clouds shrouded the peak, Mallory and Irvine disappeared. No one ever saw them alive again. Seventy-five years later, Mallory's frozen body was discovered on Mount Everest's North Face. Irvine's body is still missing. To this day, the debate continues as to whether Mallory and Irvine died on their way up to the summit, or on their way down. Other expeditions tried—unsuccessfully—to summit Everest in the 1930s and 1940s. In 1950, China invaded Tibet and closed all northern approaches to the mountain, keeping them closed until 1979. Luckily, Nepal simultaneously opened its doors, allowing foreigners to attempt Everest from the south for the first time. New Zealand beekeeper Edmund Hillary, an experienced mountaineer, rose to the challenge. As part of a British expedition, Hillary and native Nepalese climber Tenzing Norgay Sherpa finally conquered Mount Everest on the morning of May 29, 1953.

Consider the following questions that could be posed in reference to this text.

1. The title given to this selection is *Because It Is There*. Do you think this is an appropriate title? Why or why not? If you could choose another title, what would you choose?

Strategies for approaching question 1.

This question requires you to make sense of the entire story; you need to put the pieces of the story together to generate an understanding of the story's purpose. When you are asked to generate a title for a piece, you are being asked to synthesize (Strategy 7) the individual parts of the story into a greater whole. Ask yourself why the author wrote this piece; what message was he or she trying to convey? Was the purpose to warn the reader about the dangers of climbing Mount Everest? Was the purpose to encourage the reader to set challenging goals? Maybe the author just wanted to entertain the reader with an intriguing story. What do you think? Once you have thought about some of these ideas, you can decide if the title of the selection is appropriate.

In this case, the title *Because It Is There* is taken from lines 10 to 11 where the climber stated that he wanted to climb the mountain because it was there. This title does not really reflect the key ideas of this piece. Think about the most important ideas and themes in this selection (Strategy 6) and then generate a title that reflects these ideas.

The most important idea in this story is probably the fact that Mount Everest is a very dangerous and challenging mountain to climb. Some titles worth considering are

—The Monstrous Mountain

—Elusive Everest

—A Challenging Climb

What other titles can you think of that capture the key ideas of this reading selection?

2. What is the meaning of the word "cloaked" as used in line 4?

a) Discovered **b)** Masked

c) Disguised **d)** Covered

Strategies for approaching question 2.

This question requires you to look at the context surrounding the word "cloaked" to determine its meaning (Strategy 8). Given the context of the word, one of the choices provided is the best answer. Try substituting the word "cloaked" with each of the options provided:

***Discovered** in snow and ice, the mountain was considered sacred by local people.*

***Masked** in snow and ice, the mountain was considered sacred by local people.*

***Disguised** in snow and ice, the mountain was considered sacred by local people.*

***Covered** in snow and ice, the mountain was considered sacred by local people.*

Which one makes the most sense to you based on the words and sentences that surround the word "cloaked"? The first choice just does not make much sense. Did the local people find the mountain by searching through snow and ice? Not likely. Think of the summit of a very tall mountain. Usually mountains as high as Mount Everest have snow on the tops of their peaks. How would you describe snowy mountaintops? Would you say they are masked in snow, disguised in snow, or covered in snow? "Masked" and "disguised" imply that the mountain is somehow hiding, trying to conceal itself. "Covered" suggests that the mountain has a layer of snow on it. The best choice is (d) covered.

3. Why do you think the writer uses the work "luckily" (line 19) to describe the opening of Nepal's doors to foreigners wishing to summit Mount Everest from the south?

Strategies for approaching question 3.

This question requires you to make an inference (Strategy 5) about the writer's intentions. What does the word "luckily" suggest? Luckily means "by good fortune." Using this definition, then, the author writes (lines 19–20) that it was by good fortune that when China cut off access to Everest from Tibet, Nepal simultaneously (at the same time) opened its doors, allowing foreigners to attempt Everest from the south for the first time. Why would the writer suggest that this was good fortune? How do you think the author feels about allowing people to climb Mount Everest? The word "luckily" suggests that the writer thinks it was a good thing that Nepal allowed people to climb Mt. Everest, especially since climbers could no longer enter through Tibet. The author probably feels that climbing Mount Everest is an exciting and challenging journey and that people should be allowed to attempt the climb.

EXAMPLE 2

Read the following selection from *Step into the Chinese Empire.*

> The engineering wonder of Ancient China was the Great Wall. It was known as *Wan Li Chang Cheng*, or the Wall of Ten Thousand *Li* (a unit of length). The Great Wall's main length was an incredible 4,000 kilometres. Work began on the wall in the 400s BC and lasted until the AD 1500s. Its purpose was to protect China's borders from the fierce tribes who lived to the north. Despite this intention, Mongol invaders managed to breach its defences time after time. However, the Great Wall did serve as a useful communication route. It also extended the Chinese empire's control over a very long distance. The Grand Canal is another engineering project that amazes us today. It was started in the 400s BC, but was mostly built during the Sui dynasty (AD 581–618). Its aim was to link the north of China with the rice-growing regions in the south via the Chang Jiang (Yangzi) River. It is still in use and runs northwards from Hangzhou to Beijing, a distance of 1,794 kilometres.

Consider the following questions that could be posed in reference to this text.

1. Why are the words "*Wan*," "*Li*," "*Chang*," and "*Cheng*" in italics?

Strategies for approaching question 1.

To answer this question, you may need to draw on a couple of different reading comprehension strategies. First of all, if you have encountered an informational text before, you may be able to draw on your prior knowledge (Strategy 1) and recognize that the writer has put these words in italics to make them stand out. Writers sometimes use italics to draw attention to important ideas (Strategy 6). In this case, however, what you have probably noticed is that these words are not actually English words. Therefore, it is unlikely that the writer is trying to draw attention to them because of their importance. Rather, the writer has likely put these words in italics so that readers can easily recognize that the words are Chinese.

2. According to the text, what was the intended purpose of the Great Wall?

a) a communication route
b) a tourist attraction
c) a defensive structure
d) a border between China and other countries

Strategies for approaching question 2.

If you were monitoring for meaning (strategy #3) as you read this selection, this question should be fairly straightforward. It asks what was the intended (planned or designed) purpose of the Great Wall, that is, why was the Great Wall built? If you were reading carefully and making sure that you understood what you were reading, you can probably answer this question without looking back at the text. However, lines 4–5 contain the answer to this question: "*Its purpose was to protect China's borders from the fierce tribes who lived to the north*". The Wall was to provide a defensive structure to protect the Chinese from the Northern tribes. Although the Great Wall also acted as a communication route, that was not its intended purpose. Today, the Great Wall is a popular tourist attraction, but again, that was not the intended purpose. Though the Wall also allowed China to extend its control over a very long distance (lines 7–8), it was not designed as a border between China and other countries.

3. Which of the following titles would be best for this selection?

a) The Great Wall
b) Communication Routes
c) The Grand Canal
d) Feats of Engineering

Strategies for approaching question 3.

This question requires that you make sense of the entire story. When you are asked to generate a title for a piece, you are being asked to synthesize (strategy #7) the individual parts of the story into a greater whole. Why did the author write this piece; what message was he or she trying to convey? Which title best describes the entire piece or the most important idea of the story? Neither 'The Great Wall' nor 'The Grand Canal' would be appropriate as each of those titles only refers to one part of the reading. 'Communication Routes' would be a reasonable choice since both the Great Wall and The Grand Canal can be used as communication routes; however, the best title would be 'Feats of Engineering'. Both the Great Wall and the Grand Canal are introduced in this reading selection as being important engineering accomplishments. In line 1, the author states "The engineering wonder of Ancient China was the Great Wall." Then in line 8, the author states "The Grand Canal is another engineering project that amazes us today." Both of these statements draw the reader's attention to the key theme in this reading selection: engineering feats.

EXAMPLE 3

Read the following selection from *Explore! A Book of Science.*

MYSTERIOUS BLACK HOLES

Imagine a day in the future when space travel is common. Instead of telling their children to look both ways before crossing the street, parents will probably warn them: "Remember to stay away from black holes." It's good advice. Get too close to a black hole and suddenly it's like being at the mercy of a hungry vacuum cleaner. Black holes "eat" all matter that comes near them: gases, dust, and even stars. How? With fields of gravity so strong that not even light escapes them. "So how," the space-aged kids might ask their parents, "can we know where black holes are if we can't even see them?" As a black hole eats, the matter swirls around and is torn apart before it disappears. This releases energy that can be seen as light. Some of the light is pulled in by the black hole's gravity—but some escapes. This light radiates out from the black hole and shines in the shape of an oval. So an oval of light is a good warning that a black hole might be nearby. But not all black holes have light around them. That's because they have eaten all the matter near them. Remember—just because you can't see them doesn't mean they're not there! If something comes close enough, they'll suck it in. So how do kids know to stay away? Well, scientists think black holes might be at the center of galaxies. More news on that will come in the next century. For now, space travellers beware!

Answer each of the following questions that could be posed in reference to this text.

1. Why is the word "eat" (line 5) in quotation marks?

Strategies for approaching question 1.

To answer this question, you can draw on a few reading comprehension strategies. First of all, you may be able to draw on your prior knowledge (Strategy 1) and recognize that the writer has put these words in quotation marks to make them stand out. Writers will sometimes use punctuation marks to draw your attention to important ideas (Strategy 6). In this case, however, it is unlikely that the writer is trying to draw your attention to the word "eat" because of its importance. Rather, the writer has likely put the word "eat" in quotation marks so that you realize that black holes don't actually "eat" all matter that comes near them. In this situation, you may have also looked at the context (Strategy 8) surrounding the word "eat" to determine that the word was not being used in a literal sense.

2. What is the writer's primary purpose in writing this article?
   - **a)** To persuade
   - **b)** To warn
   - **c)** To inform
   - **d)** To entertain

Strategies for approaching question 2.

To determine why a writer wrote a piece, you need to synthesize (Strategy 7) the individual parts of the story into a greater whole. This question requires you to put the pieces of the story together to generate an understanding of its purpose. Ask yourself why the author wrote this piece; what message was he or she trying to convey? Was the purpose to warn the reader about the dangers of black holes? Was the writer trying to persuade the reader that black holes are dangerous? Maybe the author was just trying to be funny? In this case, the writer's primary purpose was to inform the readers about black holes. Though there was a "warning" to stay clear of dangerous black holes, a possible argument as to why black holes are dangerous, and some humour in this piece, it was primarily designed to be an informative piece. Since the selection contains facts such as "With fields of gravity so strong that not even light escapes them" (line 5), "This releases energy that can be seen as light" (line 9), and "Some of the light is pulled in by the black hole's gravity" (lines 9–10), it is most probable that the writer was trying to provide the reader with information about black holes.

USING YOUR STRATEGIES WITH POETRY

Visualizing (Strategy 4) is a strategy that is often used when reading poetry. With each of the poems in this section, try creating pictures in your mind as you read. These pictures should help you to understand the poems more clearly and to answer the questions about them more easily. Each question is followed by suggestions for applying the strategies. Before you read the suggestions, take a few minutes to generate your own response to each of the questions.

EXAMPLE 1

Like with prose, it can be helpful to activate your prior knowledge (Strategy 1) when reading a poem. Often, you can look at a title to get a sense of what a poem might be about. From there, you may start to ask yourself questions that will make you think of your own experiences.

The title of the first poem you are going to read is "Winter Worries." This title may make you think about things that happen in winter. Can you think of any problems or concerns that you have had in winter before? Do you worry about keeping warm? Have you ever had to go outside at recess on a really cold day and wished you had worn your scarf? Thinking about these sorts of things before you begin reading is like making predictions (Strategy 2) about what you are going to read.

Read the following poem by Jane W. Krows.

WINTER WORRIES

Oh, lucky, lucky, lucky me!
I'm lucky as a child can be.
When winter winds my ears would harm,
My fuzzy earmuffs keep them warm.

When ice and snow take little nips,
Warm mittens cover finger tips.
My cozy coat keeps out the breeze,
My corduroys protect my knees.

But, up to now, no clothes are sold,
To keep my nose from getting cold!

Consider the following questions that could be posed in reference to this text.

1. Why does the character in this poem feel lucky?

Strategies for approaching question 1.
This question requires you to make an inference (Strategy 5). You have to think of the most likely reason that the character in this poem feels lucky. You also need to synthesize (Strategy 7) the individual parts of the story into a greater whole. Throughout the poem, the speaker talks about how she keeps warm despite the chilly winter weather. She specifically describes how different pieces of clothing keep her warm in the winter weather. She probably feels lucky to have these pieces of clothing to keep her warm. She may also feel lucky that she can be outside enjoying winter despite the chilly weather.

2. What problem did the character in the poem encounter?

Strategies for approaching question 2.
This question requires you to understand the last two lines of the poem. By monitoring your understanding of the poem's meaning (Strategy 3), you can think about how the last idea in the poem relates to the rest of the poem. Up until the last two lines, the speaker talks about how she keeps warm despite the chilly winter weather. In particular, she refers to specific body parts that would get cold if it weren't for her warm clothing (ears, finger tips, etc.). However, in the end, she has a problem: there has not yet been a garment of clothing designed to keep her nose warm. Her problem is a chilly nose.

3. What are "corduroys" (line 8)?

Strategies for approaching question 3.
This question requires you to use context clues (Strategy 8) to figure out the meaning of a possibly unfamiliar word—"corduroys." If you look at the sentence in line 8, it says, "My corduroys protect my knees." Until this point, the speaker has been describing different pieces of clothing that help her stay warm, so corduroys are likely some type of clothing. If they are protecting her knees, it would be reasonable to assume that they are a type of pants. Corduroys are indeed pants made from a strong, ribbed, and usually cotton cloth.

Example 2

Read the following poem by Morris Bishop.

SONG OF THE POP-BOTTLERS

Pop bottles, pop-bottles
in pop shops;
The pop-bottles Pop bottles
Poor Pop drops

When Pop drops pop-bottles
Pop-bottles plop!
Pop-bottle-tops topple!
Pop mops slop!

Stop! Pop'll drop bottle!
Stop, Pop stop!
When Pop bottles pop-bottles,
Pop-bottles pop!

Consider the following questions that could be posed in reference to this text.

1. What is it about this poem that is confusing?

Strategies for approaching question 1.
To understand this poem, you need to recognize that a homonym is being used throughout it (Strategy 3). A homonym refers to two or more words that are spelled and pronounced the same but have different meanings. The homonym "pop" has three meanings in this poem: soda drink, dad, and explode. The lines "When Pop bottles pop-bottles / Pop-bottles pop!" could be re-written as "When dad bottles soda bottles / soda bottles explode!" You need to read this poem very carefully to make sure that you understand which meaning is being used in each situation.

2. What problem occurs in the first stanza?

Strategies for approaching question 2.

This question draws on your prior knowledge (Strategy 1). It requires you to recall the meaning of the word *stanza.* A stanza is a section of a poem; it consists of a series of lines arranged together in a pattern of rhythm and rhyme. In this poem, there are three stanzas. Now, to determine the problem that occurs in the first stanza, you need to understand what is happening in this poem. By monitoring your understanding of the meaning (Strategy 3), you can think about the challenge that is faced by the character in this poem. The first stanza reads, "Pop bottles, pop-bottles / in pop shops; / The pop-bottles Pop bottles / Poor Pop drops." By carefully rereading this stanza, you should recognize that the problem is revealed in the last two lines of the stanza: "The pop-bottles Pop bottles / Poor Pop drops." That is, the soda bottles that dad bottles poor dad drops. The problem that occurs in this stanza is that the father is dropping the pop that he bottles.

3. What type of figurative language is used in this poem?

Strategies for approaching question 3.

This question draws on your prior knowledge (Strategy 1). You should be familiar with the following types of figurative language[1] by the end of Grade 6.

Simile is the comparison of two unlike things using the words "like" or "as." *Her cheeks were as red as roses. His eyes were like stars in the night sky.*

Metaphor is the comparison of two unlike things without using "like" or "as." The comparison is made by saying one thing is another. In the phrase *Jamie is a rock*, the intent is to show that Jamie is calm and unyielding, not that Jamie is actually a stone of some kind.

Personification is the giving of human qualities to animals or objects. *A smiling moon.*

Alliteration is the repetition of initial consonant sounds in neighbouring words. *Sweet smell of success.*

Synecdoche is the use of a part to represent the whole. *Lend me your ears* (meaning: give me your attention).

Hyperbole is exaggeration or overstatement. *I'm so hungry I could eat a horse.*

Based on these definitions, what type of figurative language do you think is used in this poem? The correct answer is *alliteration*, in this case, using the letter "P."

---

[1] adapted from http://www.tnellen.com/cybereng/lit_terms/index.html

4. What is the meaning of the word "Pop" in the first line of the first stanza?

Strategies for approaching question 4.
This question checks to see if you understand the different meanings of the word "pop" (Strategy 3). In the first line of the first stanza, "Pop bottles, pop-bottles," "pop" means "dad."

EXAMPLE 3

Read the following poem by Dorothy Aldis.

MY NOSE

It doesn't breathe;
It doesn't smell;
It doesn't feel
So very well.

I am discouraged
With my nose:
The only thing it
Does is blows.

Generate a response to each of the following questions that could be posed in reference to this text.

1. What is wrong with the speaker in this poem?

Strategies for approaching question 1.
The person speaking in this poem has a cold. The person's nose can't smell, can't breathe, and doesn't feel very well. In fact, all the nose can do is blow. Can you visualize (Strategy 4) a red and irritated nose? Can you think of a time that you have had a cold (Strategy 1)? Can you smell anything when you are congested? Do you spend most of your time blowing your nose when you are sick?

2. What does the speaker mean when she says, "It doesn't breathe" (line 1)?

Strategies for approaching question 2.

When the speaker says "It doesn't breathe" (line 1), she is referring to the nasal congestion that can happen when you are sick. Nasal congestion often prevents you from breathing through your nose, forcing you to breathe through your mouth. Again, think of the last time that you had a cold (Strategy 1). Could you breathe through your nose? Or, did you have to breathe through your mouth?

USING YOUR STRATEGIES WITH VISUAL TEXTS

Good readers look at the pictures as well as the words on the page. Cartoons are excellent tools to give you practice with your inference skills. Remember that when you infer information from a text (Strategy 5), you connect your prior knowledge (what you already know) to the text-based information (what you are reading) to create meaning beyond what is directly stated in the text.

The following cartoons and reading comprehension questions provide you with the opportunity to practice these strategies. Each question is followed by suggestions for applying the strategies. Before you read the suggestions, take a few minutes to generate your own response to each of the questions.

EXAMPLE 1

Read the following cartoons by Corey Pandolph.

Barkeater Lake: © Corey Pandolph/Dist. by United Feature Syndicate, Inc.

Consider the following questions that could be posed in reference to this text.

1. What can you infer about Brian's attitude toward Phys Ed class? How do you know?

Strategies for approaching question 1.
Here is another example of an inference (Strategy 5) question. Based on the information presented in the cartoon strip (both in the text and in the pictures), you are asked to decide how Brian feels about Phys Ed class. In the first frame of the comic, Brian asks his teacher what his class will be doing in Phys Ed. Her response is "dodgeball." In the fourth frame, Brian asks his teacher if she hates him. Why do you think he would pose such a question to his teacher? What does such a question imply about Brian's attitude toward Phys Ed, particularly toward dodgeball? It sounds like Brian is not a fan of dodgeball. In the second line of the cartoon, Brian has gone to the nurse's office complaining that he has a stomachache. The nurse asks Brian what class he is missing and he reluctantly replies "Phys Ed." The nurse responds by saying, "What a coincidence…" (frame 7). What does she mean by this? Why might the nurse say such a thing? It sounds like Brian has a history of going to the nurse's office during Phys Ed class. Both Brian's reaction to his teacher's response and the nurse's reaction to Brian's stomachache imply that Brian does not like Phys Ed class, particularly not dodgeball.

2. What do you think a good title would be for this cartoon strip?

Strategies for approaching question 2.
This question requires you to make sense of the entire story. When you are asked to generate a title for a cartoon strip, you are being asked to synthesize (Strategy 7) the individual parts of the cartoon strip into a greater whole. Ask yourself why the cartoonist wrote this strip; what message was he trying to convey? Think of a title that describes the entire cartoon strip or the most important idea of the strip.

This cartoon strip seems to focus on Brian's attitude toward Phys Ed. Here are some titles worth considering:

—Dodgeball Blues

—The Excuse

What other titles can you think of that capture the key ideas of this reading selection?

3. David Caruso is most likely a

a) nurse **c)** teacher

c) student **d)** CSI investigator

Strategies for approaching question 3.

If you are a TV watcher, you may know the answer to this question right away. In the TV series "CSI Miami," the name of the actor who plays one of the investigators is David Caruso. If you watch this show, you might have been able to connect your previous knowledge with what you read in the comic strip (Strategy 1) to determine that David Caruso is a CSI investigator (d). However, not all students watch this show, so there must be another way to find the answer to this question. By monitoring your understanding of the meaning (Strategy 3) of this cartoon strip, you should be able to determine who David Caruso is. In the final frame, Brian says, "I hope you're prepared when CSI questions you about my dodgeball-related death." The nurse responds, "Trust me, boy—I'm always prepared for a visit from David Caruso." The conversation between these two characters is where the answer to this question can be found. Brian suggests that the nurse will be questioned by CSI investigators if he dies while playing dodgeball with a bad stomachache. Although it is a silly thought, when the nurse replies that she is ready for a visit from David Caruso, we can assume that David Caruso must be a CSI investigator.

EXAMPLE 2

Read the following cartoon by Corey Pandolph.

Barkeater Lake: © Corey Pandolph/Dist. by United Feature Syndicate, Inc.

Generate a response to each of the following questions that could be posed in reference to this text.

1. What is the meaning of the final frame?

Strategies for approaching question 1.
By monitoring your understanding of the meaning (Strategy 3) of this cartoon strip, you should be able to determine the meaning of the final frame. In the second frame, Delores suggests that the name "Dr. Toothacre" is an ironic name for a dentist. In order to understand the meaning of the final frame, you need to understand the meaning of the word ironic. Ironic means something is contrary, or opposite, to what was expected or intended. You would not expect a dentist to have a name like "Toothacre." This name sounds like "tooth-acher," suggesting its owner is someone who makes teeth feel achy. In the final frame, Delores appears to realize that when the dentist's assistant says, "I suppose it would be for other dentists," the assistant is suggesting that the dentist actually does cause aching or pain in patients' teeth. Having realized this, Dolores is understandably concerned and replies worriedly, "Wait…what?!"

2. Why is there no box around frame 3? Why would the cartoonist do this?

Strategies for approaching question 2.
This is an inference (Strategy 5) question. Based on the information presented in the cartoon strip (both in the text and in the pictures), you are asked to decide why there is no box around frame 3 and why the cartoonist might do this. What effect does the cartoonist create by omitting the box around frame 3? Did you also notice that the only images in that frame are Delores and the dentist's light? The dentist's assistant and the other images included in the previous frames are left out in frame 3. What effect does this have on you as a reader? Do you get a sense of isolation? Perhaps it draws your attention to Delores and what she must be thinking. It is likely that the cartoonist omitted the box from this frame to highlight, or bring your attention, to the frame. He may have wanted you to understand the feeling of discomfort and anxiety that Delores was feeling as she came to realize that her dentist was likely going to cause her some pain.

3. What do you think a good title would be for this cartoon strip?

Strategies for approaching question 3.

This question requires you to make sense of the entire cartoon strip. When you are asked to generate a title for a cartoon, you are being asked to synthesize (Strategy 7) the individual parts of the cartoon strip into a whole. Ask yourself why the cartoonist wrote this strip; what message was he trying to convey? Think of a title that describes the entire cartoon strip or the most important idea of the strip.

The key idea in this cartoon strip is the idea that Delores is visiting a dentist who is likely to inflict some pain or discomfort. Here are some titles worth considering:

—Dr. Toothacre

—The Visit

—Dangerous Dentist?

What other titles can you think of that capture the key ideas of this reading selection?

GENERAL TIPS FOR MULTIPLE-CHOICE EXAMS

- Skim through the entire test. How many questions are there? How much time do you have? Plan your time per question accordingly.
- Do not spend too much time on any one question. If you are having difficulty with a question, make a mark beside it and return to it later, if you have time. Often, it is better to skip a difficult question, complete the easier ones, and *then* return to the question that you skipped.
- Read each question carefully and underline key words. See if you know the answer *before* you look at the choices.
- Read the entire question and all of the choices before deciding which one best answers the question.
- If you are unsure which answer is correct, cross out any choices that you know are incorrect. Decide on the best answer from the remaining choices.
- Do not leave any questions unanswered. It is perfectly all right to guess the answer if you are stuck.
- If you have enough time, review the test, checking each of your answers.

READING TEST TIPS

- Reread parts of the passage for clarification.
- Look carefully at visual forms of information such as pictures or charts.
- If lines from the reading selection are referred to in the question, reread them before answering the question. Think about the meaning of these lines within the context of the surrounding lines as well as within the context of the whole reading selection.
- Questions are usually ordered according to the location of the answers in the selection. For instance, the answer to the first question will likely appear close to the beginning of the selection, while questions that refer to the entire passage will likely appear at the end of the set of questions.

KEY STRATEGIES FOR SUCCESS ON TESTS

NOTES

KEY STRATEGIES FOR SUCCESS ON TESTS

COMMON TYPES OF TEST QUESTIONS

To do well at school you need to:

- know the subject content
- be able show your knowledge and understanding of the content.

You can improve your performance on a test if you learn how to answer some of the most common types of exam questions. The most common types of exam question formats are multiple choice, numerical response, written response, and essay. The following information tells you about each of these question formats and makes some suggestions for how you might answer each type.

- **MULTIPLE CHOICE** – is a question where you must pick the correct ending to a statement of the correct answer from several choices. To do your best on multiple choice questions, you should try to:
  - learn important definitions, examples, and ideas
  - remember what the "exceptions to the rule" are
  - underline or circle important information that is given
  - finish the statement or answer the question before you look at the choices given to you

- **NUMERICAL RESPONSE** – is a question where you have to calculate the answer from the information given to you. To do your best on numerical response questions, you should try to:
  - **memorize** things such as the multiplication tables and formulas
  - **estimate the answer** before working out the calculation
  - **check your answer** using the related operation

- **WRITTEN RESPONSE** – is a question where you must answer in one or more sentences. To do your best on written response questions, you should try to:
  - watch for **directing words** such as “list,” “explain,” “define”
  - be certain you have answered the question asked
  - use part of the question in your answer. For example, if the question is “What are the four Rs to having a greener planet?” your answer could start with, “The four Rs to having a greener planet are reduce, reuse, recycle, and reclaim.”

- **ESSAY** – is a response that is made up of several paragraphs. To do your best on this type of question, you should try to:
  - use an organizer such as an outline or mind map to organize your thoughts
  - be sure you have an introduction, body and conclusion
  - use descriptive words to express your ideas
  - read your work over to be sure it makes sense as it moves from one idea to the next

TEST ANXIETY

Do you get test anxiety? Most students feel worried or anxious before a test. This is a normal feeling for most students. A little bit of uneasiness may sometimes help you rise to the challenge. Too much anxiety or worry interferes with your ability to do well on the test. Test anxiety may cause you to feel some of the following:

- “butterflies” in your stomach
- trouble sleeping or eating
- fear, panic, or crying
- not remembering anything or drawing a “blank” on the test

You should tell your parent or your teacher if you get these feelings most of the time when you have to write a test. If you only get these feelings sometimes, the following suggestions might help you to relax before you write your test. You can try to:
- remember that feeling a little bit uneasy before a test is a normal feeling
- take several deep breaths

- write down anything that you remember about the subject on the reverse side of your exam paper. This activity sometimes helps you to remind yourself that you <u>do</u> know something and you can do well on the test.
- say positive things to yourself such as "I can do this if I read carefully/if I start with the easy questions first/if I start with what I know/ if I stick with it"

To do well on any test, you should try to:

- be as prepared as possible
- be on time and bring whatever materials you need such as pens, pencils, and erasers
- write down the key words, definitions, or formulas on the back of the test paper before you look at the exam questions
- look at all of the exam questions before you begin answering any of them
- start with the easiest question or the question that you know you can answer correctly
- use the clues to from one question to help you with other questions or other parts of the exam
- stay in the exam room for the full time
- review your test asking yourself, "Did I do all of the questions I was supposed to do?", "Can I answer any questions now that I skipped over before?"

NOTES

PROVINCIAL ACHIEVEMENT TESTS

A Guide to Writing the Provincial Achievement Test

The *Provincial Achievement Test* section contains all of the questions from the 2000 and 2001 Provincial Achievement Tests (PATs). It is recommended that students carefully work through these exams as they are reflective of the format and difficulty level of the exam that students are likely to encounter.

THE KEY contains detailed answers that illustrate the problem-solving process for every question in this section.

When writing practice exams, students are encouraged to simulate actual Provincial Achievement Test conditions. This will help students become:

- *aware of the mental and physical stamina required to sit through an entire exam*
- *familiar with the exam format and how the course content is tested*
- *aware of any units or concepts that are troublesome or require additional study*
- *more successful in managing their review effectively*

To simulate the exam conditions students should:

- *use an alarm clock or other timer to monitor the time allowed for the exam*
- *select a quiet writing spot away from all distractions*
- *assemble the appropriate materials that are allowed for writing the exam such as pens, HB pencils, dictionary*
- *complete as much of the exam as possible within the allowable time*

In writing the practice exam students should:

- *read instructions, directions and questions carefully*
- *organize writing time according to the exam emphasis on each section*
- *highlight key words*
- *think about what is being asked*
- *plan their writing; once complete, proof for errors in content, spelling, grammar*
- *watch for bolded words such as most, least, best*
- *in multiple-choice questions, cross out any choices students know are incorrect*
- *if possible, review all responses upon completion of the exam*

2000 Provincial Achievement Test

SECTION I: NARRATIVE WRITING

Assignment

Use your imagination to write a story that the picture below has helped you think about.

When writing your story, **be sure to**

- **consider** your audience
- **focus** on your purpose
- **organize** your thoughts appropriately in sentences and paragraphs
- use **vocabulary** that is interesting and descriptive
- **edit** your work directly on your writing
- **budget** your time

SECTION II: FUNCTIONAL WRITING

The Situation

Imagine that you are a writer for your school's newspaper. Yesterday, an unusual animal called a capybara got loose when the truck taking it to the zoo was in an accident near your school. You interviewed a wildlife officer who believes that the capybara may still be somewhere nearby. After visiting the scene of the accident, you did some research on capybaras. The newspaper will be printed tomorrow, and there is just enough time to write an article.

Assignment

Write a news article that will inform the readers about what has happened and about how they can assist wildlife officers in the recapturing of the capybara.

When writing your news article, **be sure to**

- provide readers with **helpful** information
- use a **style of writing** appropriate for a news article
- use a **style of writing** appropriate for the audience
- include an **appropriate headline** for the news article

Use the following information about the accident and capybaras to help you write the article.

Notes About the Accident

What happened
- a truck overturned near the school
- the driver was shaken up but unhurt
- a capybara escaped

When
- yesterday morning

Where
- on a local road
- the capybara headed north
- the capybara could be anywhere now

Who
- the truck driver
- wildlife officers
- anyone who sees the capybara

How people can help
- note the capybara's location if they see it
- contact wildlife officers
- stay away from the capybara

Notes About Capybaras

A mother capybara and her offspring

- a mammal
- looks like a furry pig
- eats water plants and tough grasses
- a thick body and no tail
- world's largest rodent
- short legs
- can weigh up to 65 kg
- gnaws hard materials such as nuts and wood
- only defence is running or hiding in water
- often feeds on plants in shallow water
- lives in marshes and grassy areas near water
- small eyes
- lives in a warm climate
- a herbivore
- continually growing front teeth
- often grazes by cattle
- found near swamps, ponds, rivers
- runs like a horse
- few enemies
- a large, flat snout
- stays in forests and thick vegetation
- communicates by clicks, grunts, barks, whistles
- hunts for meat in some areas
- swims like a hippopotamus

Note: Among other things, you will be marked on how well you use information to support the purpose of your article.

You do not have to use all the information on this page.

You may make up additional appropriate information for the article, if you wish.

I. Read the article excerpt below and answer questions 1 to 5.

THE INSIDE STORY OF A WASPS' NEST

One winter, artist and naturalist Anker Odum found a wasps' nest in a hawthorn bush. As the temperature had been below freezing for months he knew the nest could not contain any living wasps. The only wasps to survive the winter are queens, and they hibernate away from their nest. He knew he could safely look in the nest and describe and draw what he saw. It was like trying to solve a mystery puzzle. . .

When I carefully peeled off the outer covering on one side, I found that all the inhabitants were long dead, mummified—or rather, freeze-dried—from the long cold months. The only adult wasp left in the colony lay dead just inside the entrance hole. The others were all wasp grubs and pupae, and all still in their cells. Although it was small as wasps' nests go—about the size of my fist—it contained, as far as I could estimate, about 1,000 cells. The building was in four stories, and a stalk of grass went through the whole nest, connecting the floors like a fireman's sliding pole. Apparently this had grown after the start of the colony, and the wasps had simply built around it.

1. Cells are like small "rooms" in the nest where the young wasps live. These open cells contain the eggs and the young wasps (larvae) just hatched from the eggs. In this stage the larvae look like grubs and are fed by the adult wasps.
2. This wasps' nest has four stories.
3. Each floor is suspended by a strong paper stalk.
4. A grass stalk has grown through the nest.
5. The larvae have sealed themselves in these closed cells with a white silken hood. [When the larvae are in the closed cells,] they change into adult wasps.
6. A paper-like envelope covers the nest.
7. The opening or door to the nest.

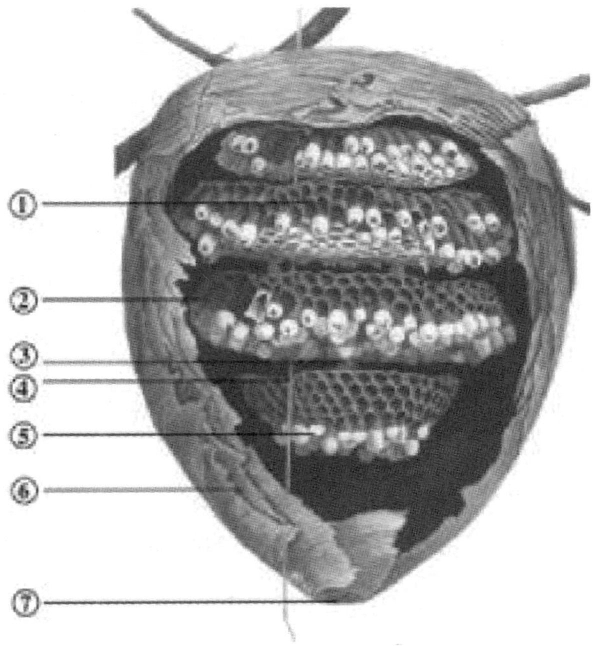

from *OWL's Summer Fun*

1. According to the article, when making sure that it is safe to look inside a wasps' nest, it is **most important** to consider the

A. time of day
B. size of the nest
C. number of wasps
D. season of the year

2. When wasps most resemble grubs, they are in the

A. egg stage
B. larva stage
C. pupa stage
D. adult stage

3. The grass stalk is in the wasps' nest because

A. the wasps stored it to use as a food source
B. the wasps brought it in and used it for support
C. it grew through the nest and the wasps left it there
D. it provided the wasps with a quick exit from the nest

4. In his description of the wasps' nest, the author suggests that the structure of a wasps' nest is **best** compared with

A. a large room
B. a busy village
C. a family residence
D. an apartment building

5. The author's activity referred to in this article is **best** described as a

A. scientific test
B. winter adventure
C. detailed investigation
D. dangerous experiment

J. PERCY PAGE

Connecting YOU to the global classroom

J. Percy Page High School is an innovative and award winning high school that provides unparalleled communication and technology opportunities to our students.

We are the first school in the country to connect to Canada's Pure Research Network along with other research institutions and universities around the world. Our state-of-the-art TeleLearning Centre gives students and staff opportunities to collaborate in real time with counterparts from anywhere in the world.

Through partnerships with business and industry, J. Percy Page is a leader in the use of technology integration in the classroom.

Register now and become part of our global learning community!

To learn more, contact:
J. Percy Page High School
2707 Mill woods road, NW
Edmonton, AB
Phone: (780) 462-3322

EDMONTON PUBLIC SCHOOLS

Superb Results *from all students*

04-6402

II. Read the poem below and answer questions 6 to 10.

BLIZZARD

The big city is rude to snow.
Trees shrug snow from their branches.
Sidewalks won't let snow stick.
Gutters refuse it too—
And so the snow melts into slush,
pretends that it never was.

Sometimes, though,
a snowfall captures the city,
sheets its statues,
tangles its streets.
Corners vanish: their policemen
whistle for them in vain.
Bus-bulls, tires spinning, snort and paw.
Even snowplows sniff at it—and stall.

A great snow hushes
the big sounds of the city.
Small sounds come out of hiding:
drops drumming on tin,
shovels strumming on narrow paths,
voices ringing in air
as clear as an empty glass.

City kids have wished all winter
for this morning.
They rush out,
hugging the snow with their bodies.

Judith Thurman

6. The stanza that **most** appeals to the sense of hearing is

A. Stanza 1
B. Stanza 2
C. Stanza 3
D. Stanza 4

7. An example of a simile is found in the words

A. "Trees shrug snow from their branches" (line 2)
B. "A great snow hushes / the big sounds of the city" (lines 15–16)
C. "voices ringing in air / as clear as an empty glass" (lines 20–21)
D. "City kids have wished all winter / for this morning" (lines 22–23)

8. The words "Bus-bulls, tires spinning, snort and paw" (line 13) are effective because they describe how buses are

A. stopping suddenly
B. making lots of noise
C. struggling in the snow
D. speeding through the snow

9. In this poem, the relationship between the city and the snow is based on

A. excitement
B. friendship
C. mistrust
D. conflict

10. During the winter, the city described in this poem

A. often gets major blizzards
B. seldom has snow that lasts
C. is prepared for large storms
D. is damaged by heavy snowfalls

III. Read the novel excerpt below and answer questions 11 to 15.

THE LIBRARY CARD

The librarian did such a good job of promoting the contest that throughout the neighbourhood, television sets were being switched off.

The Great TV Turn-Off had begun.

It was 7:00 P.M. Sunday. Brenda had already done the arithmetic. She would have to go without TV for one hundred and sixty-eight hours. Or ten thousand and eighty minutes. Or six hundred and four thousand, eight hundred seconds.

One week.

At the moment the number meant nothing to Brenda. Nothing meant anything. She was numb. Dead.

And so was her beloved TV. The voices, the laughter, the bright leaping colors—gone with the flick of a father's finger. Where moments before *Ace Monahan* was filling the screen, now there was only a flat gray nineteen-inch square. A shroud. A tombstone.

Brenda knew she was in shock. She knew this from hospital and emergency room dramas she watched. Even zebras facing lions went into shock. It was nature's way of shielding its creatures from the extremest moments of agony.

But shock was not a healthy state either—let it go on too long and you might never come out of it. That's why doctors always said of someone in shock: "Keep him warm. Raise his legs." Brenda got under the covers and put the pillow under her feet.

The red numbers of her digital clock said 7:01. Ten thousand and seventy-nine minutes to go. She groaned aloud.

By 7:20 Brenda was starting to come out of shock. And feeling really strange. Normally she was attached, connected, the stream of light a bright cord tying her to the world within the nineteen-inch tube, feeding her. Now the cord was gone, and she tumbled queasily in space.

She looked around: dresser, bookcase, beanbag chair, lavender curtains. Hanging from the closet door was a stuffed green long-legged frog. Where did that come from? She knew this room must be hers, but it felt like someone else's.

The panic hit at 7:25.

Never, never since the show began three years ago, had she missed an episode of *The Dennison Twins*, not even reruns. And now tonight's show was five minutes from over. What hilarious stunt had the zany, interchangeable brothers pulled this week? Did Robby finally get a date with Heather? Did Bobby mess things up as usual? Brenda ached to know. The not-knowing became a gnawing sharper than any hunger for ice cream or pizza. She rushed to the TV, she knelt before it. She presented her face to it, chin upthrust, eyes closed, trying to feel on her cheeks some leaking shower of photons, to capture on the nerve tips of her skin some faint electronic tickle of Robby and Bobby Dennison. With cupped hands she reached to the floor as if into a stream, scooping spilled atoms, splashing them onto her face, trying to feel . . . trying to feel. . .

Seven-thirty. The show was over. She had missed it.

And now *Pardon My Petunia* was coming on.

Jerry Spinelli

11. "The Great TV Turn-Off" (line 1) **most likely** refers to a

A. library book
B. television show
C. broken television
D. reading challenge

12. The word "tombstone" (line 11) **best** communicates the idea of

A. eeriness
B. coldness
C. hardness
D. emptiness

13. Brenda got under the covers and put the pillow under her legs in an attempt to

A. ignore the TV
B. look after herself
C. try to get some sleep
D. think about a program

14. At 7:25, Brenda panicked because she

A. forgot what program was showing
B. had not watched her favourite show
C. did not recognize her own bedroom
D. realized that only 25 minutes had passed

15. Which of the following schedules shows the times for Brenda's favourite shows?

A.

Time	Show
6:30–7:00	*The Dennison Twins*
7:00–7:30	*Ace Monahan*
7:30–8:00	*Pardon My Petunia*

B.

Time	Show
6:30–7:00	*Ace Monahan*
7:00–7:30	*The Dennison Twins*
7:30–8:00	*Pardon My Petunia*

C.

Time	Show
6:30–7:30	*Ace Monahan*
7:30–8:00	*The Dennison Twins*
8:00–8:30	*Pardon My Petunia*

D.

Time	Show
6:30–7:30	*The Dennison Twins*
7:30–8:00	*Pardon My Petunia*
8:00–8:30	*Ace Monahan*

IV. Examine the cartoon below and answer questions 16 to 18.

NANCY: © United Feature Syndicate, Inc.

16. Nancy first speaks to the boy because he is

A. unable to read the sign beside him
B. making excuses about his behaviour
C. standing around where he should not be
D. leaning against the wall wasting his time

17. To show that Nancy is embarrassed, the cartoonist draws her with

A. closed eyes
B. her finger pointed
C. lines above her head
D. her hand behind her head

18. The **main** idea of the final frame is that Nancy should

A. not be boastful
B. read all public signs
C. respect the property of others
D. not make noise in public places

V. Read the short story below and answer questions 19 to 23.

THE RICE CAKES

Years ago, in the country of Korea, lived a man named Ki Jung. He was well known throughout his village because he loved to eat rice cakes.

Indeed, it was said that the only person who might love rice cakes more than Ki Jung was Ki Jung's wife. Both were soon to discover, however, that too much love for an earthly thing can be a ruinous affair.

One particular evening in early summer, Ki Jung could hardly wait to get home from the marketplace, where he earned his living by selling brassware. All day, he had been thinking about the rice cakes a neighbour had promised to give him and his wife for supper. If only his wife weren't quite so fond of them, he thought.

When Ki Jung reached home, he banged impatiently through the front gate, calling, "The rice cakes—did our good neighbour bring them today as she promised?"

"Yes," his wife answered, "they are here on the table. All five of them."

Five! Even more than he had dared to hope for! Ki Jung's stomach was fairly hollow from hunger, and the sight of the five delicious rice cakes set his mouth to watering. He sat down on the cushion beside the table and started devouring the first cake. His wife also sat down, snatched one of the cakes, and began chewing twice as fast as her husband to make up for lost time.

All too soon, the first four cakes had disappeared, and the fifth was left sitting on the table. Ki Jung and his wife looked at it long and hard.

"I've been at the marketplace all day long, working, working, working," Ki Jung declared wearily.

His wife said nothing, but her eyes never left the rice cake.

"And the walk home from the market," Ki Jung continued, patting his belly. "Why, it seemed to take all my energy!"

Again Ki Jung's wife was silent, except for her eyes.

"Ah!" Ki Jung finally exploded. "Since you will not let me eat in peace, we will strike a bargain. The last rice cake will go to the person who can keep from talking or moving for the longest time."

"Yes," agreed his wife, with a small but triumphant smile. So the two closed their mouths tightly, gazed straight ahead, and became as rigid and still as two gray stones.

Now it happened that a thief, because he could hear no sound coming from Ki Jung's house, decided no one was at home. It wasn't until he had hoisted two sleeping mats and three quilts onto his back that he noticed Ki Jung and his wife staring straight ahead with their eyes open, not moving a muscle.

They must have frozen in terror at the sight of me, thought the thief.

Both silently watched as the thief left with Ki Jung's bowls, chopsticks, soup spoons, and Ki Jung's wife's jewelry and all her fine dresses.

Finally, she could stand it no longer. "Stop thief," she yelled. "Hah!" crowed her husband. "You spoke first. The last rice cake belongs to me!" But as he looked around the house at the spots where all his precious possessions used to be, he found he'd suddenly lost his appetite.

C. Nordhielm Wooldridge

19. Ki Jung "exploded" (line 26) because his

A. wife would not give up
B. energy had all been used up
C. wife would not stop arguing
D. stomach was so hollow with hunger

20. Ki Jung and his wife did not try to stop the intruder because they

A. were not capable of speaking
B. were protecting the rice cakes
C. wanted to eat the last rice cake
D. did not realize the man was a thief

21. The thief did not leave when he saw the couple because he

A. wanted to steal the rice cake
B. wanted to see who would eat the rice cake
C. thought they were too afraid to stop him
D. thought they could not see him

22. Ki Jung was slow to realize what had happened because he

A. was too angry with his wife
B. did not realize that anything had been stolen
C. thought only his wife's things had been stolen
D. could not think of anything except the rice cake

23. In this story, the main problem begins when

A. Ki Jung and his wife notice the thief
B. Ki Jung's wife eats faster than he does
C. Ki Jung and his wife will not share the last rice cake
D. Ki Jung's neighbour does not bring enough rice cakes

VI. Read the excerpt from a story below and answer questions 24 to 29.

TO TOUCH THE MAMMOTH

Zol, a young member of the Star Dancer tribe, has set out to touch a mammoth; a task that has only been accomplished once before.

Suddenly a shrill trumpeting pierced the morning calm. The mammoth! Zol's heart jumped to his throat.

He could still change his mind and go back. He could say he had gone out early to search for chipping rocks. But something made him go forward toward the sound. The men in his clan faced dangers every day; they did not run away. To be a Star Dancer meant to have courage.

He saw the herd over the next hill. The mammoths moved slowly along a wide stream, browsing on sedges and young willow trees. Watching them, Zol swallowed hard. They were giants! A Star Dancer could easily run under one. And the tusks! Zol's legs felt weak. What he had come to do seemed as impossible as sprouting wings and flying over the treetops. He shook his head. He could not do it. He could not touch a mammoth.

But what if he just went closer and watched? Then he could report back to Father, as a scout would. Zol moved forward.

At the stream, he crouched down and moved silently toward the herd as he had been taught. He knew mammoths had poor eyesight but very good hearing. He remembered to stay downwind so they could not smell him.

A crunching, grinding noise made Zol freeze. The willow tree next to him shook and bent over. Zol's heart hammered against his chest, but he remained perfectly still—like a quail in the underbrush. A young mammoth had strayed away from the herd and was feeding on the tree! Spotting Zol, she stopped chewing and pointed her trunk at him as if trying to smell him.

Do not run, Zol told himself. *Do not run!* The mammoth was close enough to reach out and grab him with her long trunk. He stared at the monstrous pointed tusks that curved out at him. The mammoth began to chew again, slowly grinding up the fresh willow shoots in her giant teeth.

Then she took a step toward Zol, stretching out her hairy trunk. Zol closed his eyes and held his breath. Something touched his hair. A tingle zapped through Zol's body like lightning. Then he felt a blast of her warm, smelly breath on his face.

A blaring cry split the air so suddenly that Zol screamed, too. He clapped his hand over his mouth, wild-eyed with fear. The young mammoth tossed her head, trumpeted an answering call, and lumbered off to follow the herd.

Zol collapsed like a skin without bones. He crawled to the stream and splashed water on his face. Drinking from cupped hands, he felt the sun on his back.

"I did not touch the mammoth," he said to the chuckling stream, "but the great mammoth touched *me*." A smile of wonder stretched across Zol's face. "And I did not run away!"

Patricia Nikolina Clark

24. The word "shrill" (line 1) means

A. sharp
B. gentle
C. distant
D. gradual

25. Zol set out to touch a mammoth in order to

A. become accepted by the tribe
B. prove that he was courageous
C. show that he was able to track mammoths
D. find out where the mammoths were located

26. The mammoths' weakest sense was their sense of

A. sight
B. taste
C. smell
D. touch

27. The young mammoth encountered Zol because

A. she followed Zol
B. she wandered near Zol
C. Zol made a lot of noise
D. Zol had nowhere to hide

28. The words "*Do not run!*" (line 23) are in italics in order to emphasize what Zol was

A. ordering
B. thinking
C. shouting
D. whispering

29. The expression "collapsed like a skin without bones" (line 33) suggests that Zol

A. had been injured by the mammoth
B. had been frightened by his encounter
C. was feeling exhausted, hungry, and thirsty
D. was hiding in case the mammoth returned

VII. Read the passage below and answer questions 30 to 34.

MAKING BUTTER

Do you like to spread <u>coalesced</u> fat droplets on your bread? If you do, you can make some sandwiches with the results of this experiment.

You'll need:

300 mL (½ pint) whipping cream

a small glass jar with a tight cover

1. Take the cream out of the refrigerator and let it stand for about 10 minutes so that it warms up slightly.
2. Pour the cream into the jar until the jar is one-third full.
3. Screw on the lid and make sure it doesn't leak.
4. Hold the jar in one hand and shake it in a figure-eight motion. (You'll have to keep shaking it for about 20 minutes, so it might be a good idea to have a helper available to take over in case your arm gets tired.)
5. Watch the cream change form. It will become foamy and almost look like it's whipping, but after a while, very tiny granules of butter will start to form.
6. When the granules are the size of apple seeds, stop shaking.
7. Carefully drain off the liquid—it's buttermilk and very good to drink.
8. Wash the butter granules in cold water to rinse off any remaining buttermilk.
9. Put the butter granules in a plastic or wooden dish and pack them together with a wooden spoon. If you like salty butter, add a little salt and squish it into the butter with your wooden spoon. Make sure it's worked in evenly.
10. Form your butter into any shape you like, then put it into the refrigerator to harden.

How does it work?

Cream is very tiny fat droplets permanently floating in water. If enough of those droplets can be forced together, they'll form globules of butter and separate from the water. This is called <u>coalescing</u>.

Mellow Yellow

You might notice that your butter is darker or lighter than the butter you usually get in the store. That's because the colour of pure butter depends on the kinds of cows the milk came from and what they ate. But when people buy butter, they expect it to be a uniform golden colour, so dairies usually dye it with food colouring.

from *The Jumbo Book of Science*

30. The jar no longer needs to be shaken when the

A. cream has become foamy
B. cream has warmed up slightly
C. granules of butter start to form
D. granules are the size of apple seeds

31. In this passage, the numbers 1 to 10 are used to

A. show that the instructions are simple
B. indicate how long each step should take
C. identify which steps are the most important
D. ensure that the instructions are followed in order

32. According to the passage, salt may be added to butter in order to

A. keep the butter fresh
B. make the butter smooth
C. change the taste of the butter
D. improve the colour of the butter

33. The underlined words "coalesced" and "coalescing" refer to

A. cooling down
B. coming together
C. mixing with butter
D. mixing with water

34. The section entitled "Mellow Yellow" is in a box because it

A. gives interesting extra information
B. explains the process of making butter
C. summarizes the main points of the passage
D. contains the most important information on the page

VIII. Read the poem below and answer questions 35 to 38.

THE GREENHORN ON SKIS

The world was a quiet white world
with diamonds on the lawn
when a greenhorn fastened boots to skis
and faced the lazy dawn.
He wore a sea-green jacket;
a white toque squeezed his head.
He was topped off with a pompom
like a cherry ripe and red.
If you've ever watched a day-old colt
tottering, knobby-kneed,
you will have a fair idea
of how that greenhorn skied.
He bumbled down the driveway
with erratic starts and stops.
He wildly lurched to starboard
and used the poles for props.
Then he anchored them in the crusted snow
and leaned on them so hard
that his feet zipped out ahead of him . . .
his sky, I'm sure, was starred.
He floundered on his back for a while
like an octopus in pain
until he managed to heave himself
upon his feet again.
His right foot began advancing;
his left one chose retreat.
The greenhorn was torn between them
for east and west don't meet.
He lay among the diamonds
and chortled aloud to his mitts,
"Tomorrow I'll tell my gym coach
that at last I've done the splits."

Myra Stilborn

35. The words "tottering" (line 10), "bumbled" (line 13), "lurched" (line 15), and "zipped" (line 19) suggest that the skier was

A. careless
B. unsteady
C. travelling quickly
D. barely moving

36. The skier's "sky . . . was starred" (line 20) because the

A. sky was very bright
B. skier bumped his head
C. snow sparkled like diamonds
D. skier lay on the snow until night

37. This poem presents a "greenhorn" as a person who

A. is weak and unathletic
B. is scared to try new things
C. has little skill and experience
D. likes to dress in funny clothes

38. The purpose of this poem is to

A. convince the reader
B. inform the reader
C. amuse the reader
D. warn the reader

IX. Read the novel excerpt below and answer questions 39 to 42.

STORY WITHOUT WORDS

Classical ballet is a form of dance that tells a story without words. The dancing is done mostly to the accompaniment of classical music by composers like Tchaikovsky, Stravinsky, and Ravel.

The very structured movements of ballet force the body to do things it was not meant to do. Legs have to turn out from the hip; the back has to arch gracefully; one pointed foot has to support the whole body.

There are five basic standing positions in ballet and about 50 traditional movements. All of these must be practised over and over and over.

Ballet started in Italy about 500 years ago. It became popular in France as a special form of entertainment for King Louis XIV. All the steps and other aspects of ballet received French names, which are still used today in every country. For example, the *barre* is the wooden rod that dancers hold when they do warm-up exercises; *pliés* (knee bends) and *jetés* (leaps) are two of the movements; a *pas de deux* is a dance for two people.

Ballet also became popular in the Soviet Union. Soviet male dancers added high kicks and jumps to the graceful movements. People who think that male ballet dancers are sissies probably don't know that most ballet dancers are stronger and fitter than football quarterbacks.

Marcia L. Kaye

Basic Positions

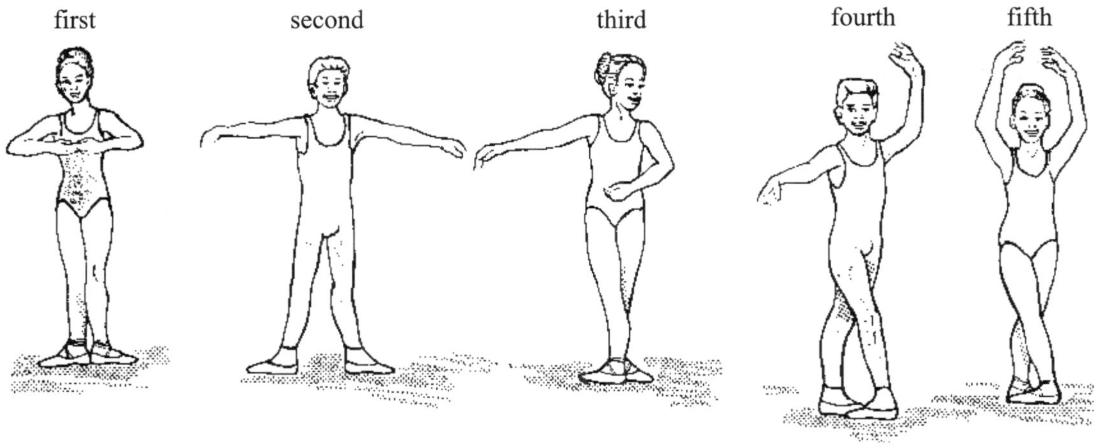

39. Ballet began in

A. Italy
B. France
C. the Soviet Union
D. the United States

40. Ballet terms are French **most likely** because

A. ballet first became popular in France
B. ballet was a traditional dance in France
C. many people understand French words
D. classical music composers wrote in French

41. The illustrations are intended to show that in ballet

A. each basic dance position is unique
B. males and females use different positions
C. dancers move gracefully from one position to the next
D. arm placement is the most important part of each position

42. "Story Without Words" is a good title because

A. classical music has no words
B. people of different languages can dance
C. ballet is a special form of entertainment
D. ballet dancers communicate through movement

X. Read the passage below and answer questions 43 to 47.

THE COMICS

Who and what are behind the comic strips in your newspaper? Meet Lynn Johnston, whose comic strip "For Better or For Worse" appears in more than 1 500 newspapers around the world.

Q. Where do you get your ideas for the strip?

A. I'm on RECORD all the time, getting ideas. "Spot" ideas work well, like the image of a son talking on the phone all day but never saying a word to his mother. He's talked out!

Q. Do you only create the artwork?

A. Some cartoonists work with writers, but I do both the writing and the drawing. There's only a limited space for the message and I am very demanding of myself. I write and rewrite the words for each strip. By the time I reach the last panel, I need a punch line or a pun or a strong remark.

Q. How do you draw the panels in your strip?

A. I use a template (a pattern) and draw the four panels on my board. Since my hands perspire a lot, I wear a cotton glove (with the fingers cut off) to keep the cartoon clean. In each panel, I sketch the drawings and print the words in pencil. Then I use ink and two different pens to write over the words and finish the picture. If I make a mistake in the drawing, I use white animation paint to cover it. When the paint is dry I can draw over it. Sometimes I cut out a new panel and glue it over the one with the mistake.

Q. How far ahead do you work?

A. I work on the daily strips six weeks ahead of when they'll appear in the newspapers. The weekend coloured strips are done eight weeks ahead. That means at Christmas, I'm already thinking about the Easter strips.

Q. We hear about "writer's block." Is there such a thing as "cartoonist's block"?

A. There are dry times when I have no ideas. It's good that I'm always working so far ahead on the strip, just in case it happens. Sometimes I stop working and take a long walk. Or I read something funny to get in a good mood. Even sleep can help. Sleep can be part of the creative process.

Q. Can you offer any tips to young people who would like to become comic-strip artists?

A. Practise a lot. Copying isn't bad unless you say someone else's work is yours. Be honest. Develop your own style. A cartoonist's style is as personal as his or her signature. It takes a long time to get both the way you want them. Learn from others. I learned a lot from my favourites, like the artists in *Mad* magazine. And never say "I'm good," say "I could be better."

Linda Granfield

43. The format of this passage shows that it is

A. an interview
B. an outline
C. a report
D. a play

44. Lynn Johnston says she is "on RECORD all the time" (line 5) because she is always

A. writing and rewriting each panel
B. gathering thoughts for later use
C. working to meet deadlines
D. developing her own style

45. Lynn Johnston wears a glove when she works in order to

A. avoid smudging her work
B. avoid making mistakes
C. keep her hand warm
D. keep her hand clean

46. The expression "'cartoonist's block'" (line 23) refers to a cartoonist

A. planning ahead
B. feeling uncreative
C. being unable to sleep
D. reading something funny

47. Which quotation from Lynn Johnston shows that she considers attitude to be an important factor in becoming successful?

A. "I do both the writing and the drawing" (line 8)
B. "Sleep can be part of the creative process" (lines 26–27)
C. "Copying isn't bad unless you say someone else's work is yours" (line 29)
D. "And never say 'I'm good,' say 'I could be better'" (lines 32–33)

XI. Examine the cartoon below and answer questions 48 to 50.

© Lynn Johnston Productions Inc./Dist. By United Features Syndicate

48. The word that is closest in meaning to "MOPING" (first frame) is

A. sulking
B. whining
C. complaining
D. daydreaming

49. Elizabeth's expression in the third frame suggests that she

A. does not believe her father
B. does not want to listen to her father
C. is really upset about her haircut
D. is considering her problem in a new way

50. The **main** point of this cartoon is that we should

A. keep our problems in perspective
B. never become upset by our problems
C. be more concerned about others than ourselves
D. be more aware of what is happening in the world

2001 Provincial Achievement Test

Some readings, questions, and solutions are common to both the 2000 and 2001 provincial achievement tests. The common readings, questions, and solutions from the 2000 Provincial Achievement Test are not repeated here as part of the 2001 Provincial Achievement Test for Grade 6 Language Arts.

SECTION I: NARRATIVE WRITING

Assignment

Use your imagination to write a story that the picture below has helped you think about.

When writing your story, **be sure to**

- **consider** your audience
- **focus** on your purpose
- **organize** your thoughts appropriately in sentences and paragraphs
- use **vocabulary** that is interesting and descriptive
- **edit** your work directly on your writing
- **budget** your time

SECTION II: FUNCTIONAL WRITING

The Situation

You are a writer for your school's newspaper. Recently a group of students, parents, and a teacher returned from a school trip to St. John's, Newfoundland. You interviewed some of the students, one of the parents, and the teacher. They told you about why they went to Newfoundland and about some of the interesting things they did on the trip. You have also done some research on Newfoundland. Now you are ready to write your news article.

Assignment

Write a news article that will inform the readers about the purpose of the school trip to Newfoundland and about some of the interesting things the group did while it was there. Include an appropriate headline for the article.

When writing your news article, **be sure to**

- provide readers with **information** that will support the purpose of the news article
- use a **style of writing** appropriate for a news article
- use a **style of writing** appropriate for the audience

Use the following information provided to assist in your writing.

Notes About the Trip

What happened?
- school trip to St. John's, Nfld.
- visited sites in and around St. John's

Why did the group go?
- to experience culture and lifestyle from a different region of Canada

Where did the group go?
- City of St. John's
- St. John's Middle School
- various communities in Newfoundland

Who was involved?
- Grade 6 students, classroom teacher, parents
- school families from St. John's Middle School

How was the trip funded?
- government-sponsored youth exchange program

How did the group travel?
- travel by air to Halifax, N.S.
- Marine Atlantic Ferry to Argentia, Nfld.
- tour bus to surrounding areas
- travel by air to Alberta

Facts About Newfoundland	*Highlights of the Trip*
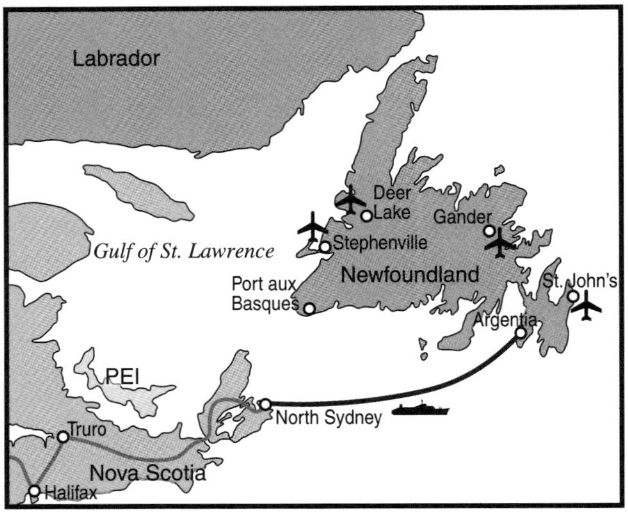 • newest province in Canada (joined 1949) • rugged landscape and rocky coastline • fishing, forestry, mining, and oil production are major industries • many freshwater lakes and rivers • most communities located along the coast • children must attend school from 7 to 16 years of age	• provincial museum of Newfoundland and Labrador • riding the ferry and seeing ships • going out on the ocean to look for whales • meeting many kind and generous people in Newfoundland • helping to uncover artifacts at the Colony of Avalon Archaeology Site near St. John's • going to school with the Grade 6 class of St. John's Middle School • community supper and family dance at St. John's Middle School • visiting a lighthouse

You do not have to use all the information provided on this page

You may include additional appropriate information for your article

I. Read the article excerpt below and answer questions 1 to 5.

THE INSIDE STORY OF A WASPS' NEST

The article excerpt THE INSIDE STORY OF A WASPS' NEST and questions 1 to 5 are not reprinted here as they are part of the 2000 Provincial Achievement Test included in this resource.

II. Read the poem below and answer questions 6 to 10.

THE ATTIC

Where curtains gray
As winter clouds
Wrap windows with
Their lacy shrouds
And hide the glass,
Some dark, some clear:
This is my place to dream—
Right here.

Where Summer sleeps
On sun blocked floor,
Where hinges creak
On wooden door,
Where walls are hung
With grandpa's gear:
This is my place to dream—
Right here.

Where webs hang down
And dust grows up
And a single fly
In an old chipped cup
Sings buzz-buzz-buzz
As sharp as fear:
This is my place to dream—
Right here.

And when I'm old
And far away
The smell of dust,
The look of gray
A pane of glass
Both dark and clear
Will bring me back to dream—
Right here.

Jane Yolen

6. In this poem, the word "shrouds" (line 4) refers to

A. the sky
B. a covering
C. the sunlight
D. a secret place

7. The poet's **main** purpose for using the phrase "Right here" at the end of each stanza is to

A. mark the end of a sentence
B. communicate a satisfactory ending
C. emphasize the importance of the setting
D. provide a rhyme for the last word of each stanza

8. In this poem, the poet thinks of the attic **mainly** as

A. a place to rest
B. a special place
C. cluttered and messy
D. dark and frightening

9. In context, the phrase "Where walls are hung" (line 13) means that the walls are

A. lined with objects
B. held with ropes
C. broken down
D. tied together

10. The narrator expects that when she is older, she will

A. visit the attic often
B. carefully look in the attic
C. compare other places with the attic
D. sometimes be reminded of the attic

III. Read the novel excerpt below and answer questions 11 to 15.

The article excerpt THE LIBRARY CARD and questions 11 to 15 are not reprinted here as they are part of the 2000 Provincial Achievement Test included in this resource.

IV. Examine the cartoon below and answer questions 16 to 18.

HÄGAR THE HORRIBLE

Frame 1

Frame 2

Frame 3

Frame 4

Frame 5

Frame 6

16. The words "DECISIONS, DECISIONS, DECISIONS!!" are used in frame 2 in order to make the reader

A. feel disappointed with the Viking
B. become angry with the Viking
C. sympathize with the Viking
D. laugh at the Viking

17. In frame 4, the Viking's expression is one of

A. hesitation
B. confusion
C. excitement
D. seriousness

18. Which of the following comments **best** establishes humour in this cartoon?

A. "The job of a viking chieftain is full of stress!"
B. "Important decisions! Tough decisions!"
C. "Decisions only **I** can make!"
D. "Do you want bacon and eggs or pancakes for breakfast?"

V. Read the short story excerpt below and answer questions 19 to 23.

from I SURVIVED THE TITANIC

Ruth Becker was 12 years old when she set sail on the R.M.S. Titanic. This is her true story.

. . . An inspection of the ship revealed the worst. The iceberg had bashed the hull and water was gushing in. Six of sixteen compartments were flooding. The *Titanic* was doomed.

At 12:02 A.M. Captain Smith fired orders to the crew. Radio operators telegraphed nearby ships for help.

Stokers deep below deck continuously shoveled coal into giant boilers, supplying power to keep the pumps running and the lights lit. Stewards started knocking on cabin doors, alerting sleeping travelers of trouble.

Some passengers had been awakened by a slight jolt when the *Titanic* struck the iceberg. A curious few discovered tons of ice on one of the decks. Some men even began a playful ice fight.

Deep in the forward section a few people realized something was seriously wrong. Postal workers lugged bags of sopping wet mail to a higher deck. Water swirled on the floors of some third-class cabins.

"My mother had just gone to bed . . . when she was awakened by the engines stopping," described Ruth. "Then she heard a pounding noise." One steward reassured her it was nothing. Their own steward, however, told her to get up on deck—that the ship was sinking. "So she awakened me and we put on our clothes, stockings, and our coats over our nightclothes and went to the upper deck. It was almost like a dream—everything was very orderly and very quiet. We had to climb five flights of stairs to a room full of women. They were all weeping—in all states of dress and undress. Everyone was frightened—no one knew what would happen to them. But I was never scared. I was only excited. I never for one minute thought we would die."

Officers were lowering lifeboats. Orders were to load women and children first.

But . . . there were too few lifeboats! They had space for only 1,178 of the 2,228 passengers and crew aboard. The only hope for the others was help from another ship...

On deck, the crew fired distress rockets. The orchestra played lively tunes to calm passengers. Mrs. Becker sent Ruth back to their cabin for blankets. Ruth returned to find officers loading women and children into a nearby lifeboat. "One officer grabbed my sister, another carried my brother into a lifeboat and yelled, 'All full!' My mother screamed. . . . They let mother on, but they left me behind.

"My mother yelled at me to take the next lifeboat, and before I knew it, an officer picked me up and dumped me into a boat." Seconds later, the crew lowered Ruth's lifeboat, #13, down 50 feet. As it neared the sea, jets of water spewed from the *Titanic*, pushing Ruth's boat directly beneath the next lifeboat, #15, being lowered. People shouted desperately for someone to stop lowering #15, but it kept coming. An instant before the lifeboats collided, a man cut #13's lines. Freed just in time, the boat swung away from the ship.

Jennifer A. Kirkpatrick

19. The phrase "Captain Smith fired orders" (line 6) means that the captain

A. tried to keep the passengers informed
B. sent messages to nearby ships
C. gave the crew jobs to do
D. set off emergency flares

20. Mrs. Becker was awakened by

A. a slight jolt
B. a pounding noise
C. the cabin steward
D. the stopping of the engines

21. Ruth recalls that as the *Titanic* was sinking, she was **mainly** feeling

A. excited
B. amused
C. perturbed
D. frightened

22. The sentence "The only hope for the others was help from another ship" (line 28) creates a sense of

A. mystery
B. suspense
C. frustration
D. desperation

23. The reason that people shouted to stop lowering lifeboat #15 was that

A. Ruth was not aboard yet
B. another lifeboat was below it
C. it was still 50 feet from the water
D. water was spewing from the *Titanic*

VI. Read the story excerpt below and answer questions 24 to 29.

The article excerpt TO TOUCH THE MAMMOTH and questions 24 to 29 are not reprinted here as they are part of the 2000 Provincial Achievement Test included in this resource.

VII. Read the passage below and answer questions 30 to 34.

The article excerpt MAKING BUTTER and questions 30 to 34 are not reprinted here as they are part of the 2000 Provincial Achievement Test included in this resource.

VIII. Read the poem below and answer questions 35 to 38.

NO ONE HEARD HIM CALL

He went down to the woodshed
To put his bike away.
There was no moon. There were no stars.
He ran the whole dark way.
And when he hurried back again
The porch light had gone out!
He couldn't find the doorknob,
So then he gave a shout.

It wasn't very loud, though,
And no one heard him call.
He pounded with his knuckles;
Still no one came at all.
But then where he was standing
A *light* came streaming wide:
"My goodness, is that you?" she said.
And he was safe inside!

Dorothy Aldis

35. In the poem, the sentences "There was no moon. There were no stars" (line 3) are used to develop

A. character
B. mystery
C. setting
D. plot

36. The boy in the poem is **most anxious** about

A. being alone in the dark
B. running around outside
C. losing his way in the dark
D. seeing that the porch light is out

37. The sentence "Still no one came at all" (line 12) establishes a sense of

A. hope
B. regret
C. danger
D. suspense

38. The woman in the poem says, "'My goodness, is that you?'" (line 15) because she is

A. upset that the boy has hurt himself
B. unable to see the boy because it is too dark
C. annoyed that the boy is pounding on the door
D. surprised that the boy is outside by himself in the dark

IX. Read the experiment below and answer questions 39 to 42.

WHY DOES POPCORN POP?

Have you ever wondered about what would happen if you put uncooked kernels of corn from corn on the cob into the microwave? Would they pop and make great popcorn? The bad news is that they would just make a mess of your microwave. The good news is that popcorn, whose proper name is *popping corn*, is a special breed of corn that will explode to 30 to 40 times its original size when you heat it.

Only popping corn will pop. The secret to its pop is a drop of water found in each kernel. As each kernel is heated, the drop of water turns to steam (just as boiling water turns to steam). The steam is energy that breaks the hard kernel, and out pops popcorn!

HOW TO GET THE BEST POPS FROM YOUR POPCORN

An Experiment

Purpose

To determine whether dry or wet popcorn pops better.

Materials

750 ml unpopped popcorn
cookie sheet
medium bowl
plastic sandwich bag
colander
frying pan, lid, and
vegetable oil *or*
hot-air popcorn popper

Procedure

1. Place 250 ml popcorn on cookie sheet and leave in an oven at 95°C for 60 minutes.
2. Place 250 ml popcorn in bowl with 500 ml water for 60 minutes. After 60 minutes, drain the popcorn in a colander.
3. Leave 250 ml popcorn in a plastic bag for 60 minutes.
4. Pop each of the three batches of popcorn separately.
5. Which batch of popcorn made the biggest kernels of popcorn? Which batch made the smallest kernels?
6. Measure how much popcorn each batch made using a measuring cup. Which batch made the most popcorn? Which batch made the least popcorn?

What Happened?

The popcorn that was soaked in water made the biggest kernels of popped popcorn as well as the largest amount of popcorn. This is because the soaking process added water to the kernel. The more water there is, the more steam is created in cooking, making the kernels pop better. The popcorn that was dried out in the oven lost most of that drop of water that turns to steam during popping. The dried popcorn kernels made smaller kernels of popped popcorn and were more likely to be duds (unpopped kernels). Therefore, they produced the smallest amount of popped popcorn. The popcorn that was left in a plastic bag made medium-sized kernels of popped popcorn and an average amount, as it was neither dried nor soaked.

From *The Jumbo Book of Science*

39. The questions at the beginning of the experiment (lines 1 and 2) are intended to

A. invite the reader to reply
B. interest the reader in the topic
C. determine what the reader knows
D. encourage the reader to eat popcorn

40. The words "*popping corn*" (line 4) are in italics to indicate

A. the correct pronunciation
B. the correct term
C. an abbreviation
D. a brand name

41. The purpose of using a colander, as described in Procedure 2, is to

A. prevent the kernels from drying out
B. hold the kernels while they are popping
C. hold the kernels while the water is drained
D. make sure the kernels are thoroughly soaked

42. Which of the following charts summarizes the results of this experiment?

A.

	Results	
Condition of popcorn	Size of kernel	Amount of popcorn produced
Dried	*medium*	*most*
Soaked	*biggest*	*average*
Left in Bag	*smallest*	*least*

B.

	Results	
Condition of popcorn	Size of kernel	Amount of popcorn produced
Dried	*medium*	*most*
Soaked	*smallest*	*average*
Left in Bag	*biggest*	*least*

C.

	Results	
Condition of popcorn	Size of kernel	Amount of popcorn produced
Dried	*smallest*	*least*
Soaked	*medium*	*average*
Left in Bag	*biggest*	*most*

D.

	Results	
Condition of popcorn	Size of kernel	Amount of popcorn produced
Dried	*smallest*	*least*
Soaked	*biggest*	*most*
Left in Bag	*medium*	*average*

X. Read the article excerpt below and answer questions 43 to 47.

Of course, as we all know, the Vikings didn't have newspapers. But if they had, we're sure that they all would have been reading this article.

FIGHTING FIT

Our powerful longships are without a doubt the finest fighting ships in all of Europe! Here a master boatbuilder tells *The Viking News* just what makes them so special.

1. The first thing any ship needs is a strong keel—it's the backbone that supports everything else.

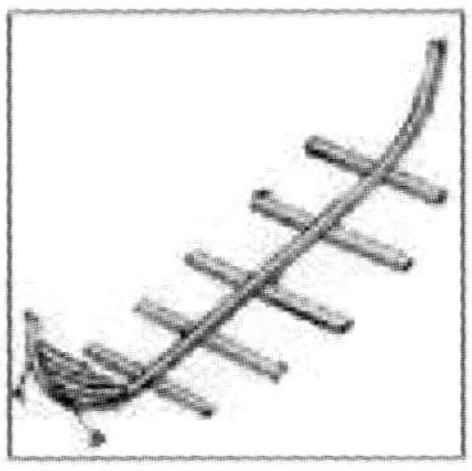

Keel: Strong and long.

For a longship's keel, I will use only the very best-quality oak, which I cut from the trunk of a single straight tree.

2. The next thing is the hull, and it's the hull's unique shape that makes the longship so formidable.

The base of the hull should be made as flat as possible. This is why our longships can sail in far shallower waters than other warships—allowing our warriors to raid almost any town near a coast or river.

Each plank of the hull is cut as thinly as possible. This makes the longship incredibly light, which means, of course, that it's also stunningly fast—nothing can beat it for speed!

3. Once the hull is in place, the deck is laid, using strong, close-fitting planks.

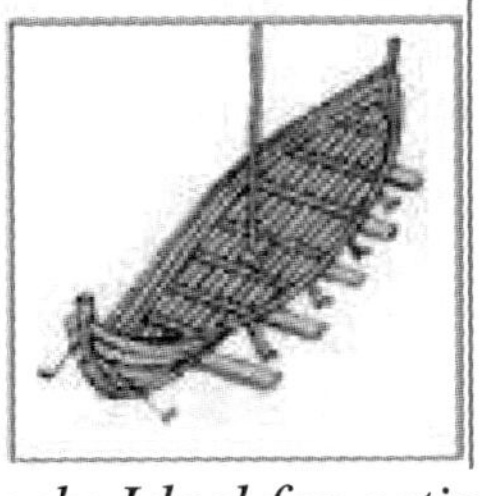

Deck: Ideal for action.

Longships are built for fighting, so the deck is kept free of anything that might get in the crew's way. Many of our longships don't even have benches for the rowers to sit on. Instead, they make do with the wooden chests used for storing their weapons and armor.

4. After this, the mast is added. Like the keel, it is fashioned from a single tree trunk.

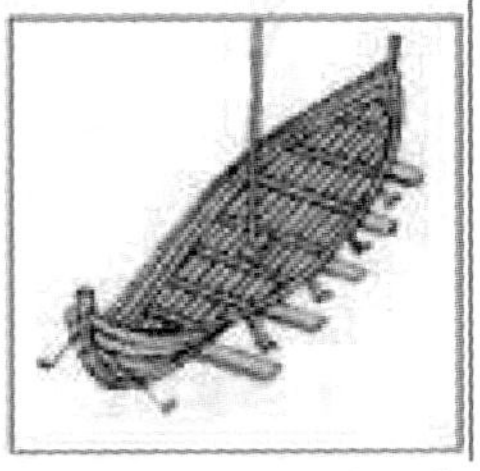

Mast: Easy to take down.

The mast must be tall enough to support the huge sail, and yet have the strength to withstand the fiercest ocean gale.

It must also be easily raised and lowered so that the crew can switch from sail to oar at a moment's notice—vital for a quick getaway when the wind's in the wrong direction.

5. Our longships are envied throughout Europe, and rightly so! But even the finest ship is worthless without a good crew. People fear our ships because of the warriors who sail them. Viking men are fine sailors, powerful oarsmen, and bold fighters—it is they who make our ships so deadly.

Rachel Wright

43. A longship must have a strong keel because the keel

A. allows a longship to land on rocky beaches
B. allows a longship to sail in rough seas
C. supports the longship's huge sail
D. holds the longship together

44. A longship is extremely fast because the

A. mast can be raised and lowered quickly
B. deck is flat and kept free of obstacles
C. crew are ready to row in an instant
D. planks of the hull are cut thinly

45. The order in which the parts of a Viking longship are assembled is

A. keel, hull, deck, mast
B. keel, mast, deck, hull
C. keel, hull, mast, deck
D. keel, deck, hull, mast

46. The reasons that Viking longships are "envied throughout Europe" are that they

A. are fast, can travel in shallow water, and can sail in storms
B. can sail in storms, have a flat deck, and have a backbone
C. have a tall mast, are fast, and are made from a single tree
D. can travel in shallow water and are inexpensive

47. An example of a statement of opinion is found in the words

A. "longships are without a doubt the finest fighting ships"
B. "I will use only the very best-quality oak"
C. "Many of our longships don't even have benches"
D. "The mast must be tall enough to support the huge sail"

XI. Examine the cartoon below and answer questions 48 to 50.

See the cartoon NANCY and questions 48 to 50 are not reprinted here as they are part of the 2000 Provincial Achievement Test included in this resource.

Answers and Solutions
2000 Provincial Achievement Test

1.	**D**	**11.**	**D**	**21.**	**C**	**31.**	**D**	**41.**	**A**
2.	**B**	**12.**	**D**	**22.**	**D**	**32.**	**C**	**42.**	**D**
3.	**C**	**13.**	**B**	**23.**	**C**	**33.**	**B**	**43.**	**A**
4.	**D**	**14.**	**B**	**24.**	**A**	**34.**	**A**	**44.**	**B**
5.	**C**	**15.**	**B**	**25.**	**B**	**35.**	**B**	**45.**	**A**
6.	**C**	**16.**	**C**	**26.**	**A**	**36.**	**B**	**46.**	**B**
7.	**C**	**17.**	**C**	**27.**	**B**	**37.**	**C**	**47.**	**D**
8.	**C**	**18.**	**A**	**28.**	**B**	**38.**	**C**	**48.**	**A**
9.	**D**	**19.**	**A**	**29.**	**B**	**39.**	**A**	**49.**	**D**
10.	**B**	**20.**	**C**	**30.**	**D**	**40.**	**A**	**50.**	**A**

THE INSIDE STORY OF A WASPS' NEST

1. D

Line 3 of the article tells the reader that it is safe to look in the wasps' nest because the "*only wasps to survive the winter are queens, and they hibernate away from their nest.*" Wasps cannot survive below freezing weather regardless of the time of day (A), size of the nest (B), or number of wasps (C). According to the article, when making sure that it is safe to look inside a wasps' nest, it is most important to consider the season of the year.

2. B

This question can be answered by reading carefully. Number 1 in the diagram labels the cells in the wasp nest. The description of number 1 contains the answer to this question. It tells us that when wasps are in the larval stage, they "look like grubs."

3. C

Lines 12 to 13 provide the answer to this question. They say that the grass stalk "had grown after the start of the colony, and the wasps had simply built around it." Therefore, the wasps did not use it as a food source (A) or as a quick exit from the nest (D). We know that they did not bring it in and use it for support (B) because the stalk grew after the start of the colony.

The grass stalk is in the wasps' nest because it grew through the nest and the wasps left it there.

4. D

It is necessary to know the different characteristics of the answers in order to compare them with the author's description of the wasps' nest. In lines 11 to 12, the writer describes the wasps' nest as having four storeys ("stories").

A. A large room does not have different storeys.

B. A busy village would not generally be described using the word "stories" because in a village, there are a number of free-standing buildings, some of which may have multiple storeys and some may not. Note that you are looking for the best answer. This is not the best answer.

C. A family residence may have more than one storey, but it generally does not have four stories. Again, note that you are looking for the best answer. This is not the best answer.

D. An apartment building can be four storeys high; therefore, this is the best answer.

5. C

The word "best" in this question is bolded. This means that one or more answers may be correct, but you must choose the best answer out of the choices provided.

The author's activity in this article would not be described as a scientific test (A) because nothing is being tested. The wasps' nest is being examined. Referring to this activity as a "winter adventure" (B) is possible because the activity does take place in the winter, however, an "adventure" usually involves more activity and excitement. This is not the best answer. The author's activity would not be described as a "dangerous experiment" (D). Anker Odum is not carrying out an experiment, and there are no wasps present to make this activity dangerous.

This article is best described as a detailed investigation (C) because Anker Odum has written about investigating the wasps' nest and making notes on its structure. The article is very detailed and informative.

BLIZZARD

6. C

A stanza is like a paragraph that divides a poem into sections.

A. Stanza 1 has words that suggest rejection: rude, shrug, refuse. There is nothing to describe sound.

B. Stanza 2 is full of action words: captures, sheets, tangles, vanish, whistle, spinning, snort, paw, sniff, stall. Some of these words suggest sound, but all of them suggest activity.

C. Stanza 3 is all about sound: hushes, big sounds, small sounds, drumming, strumming, ringing. Some of these words suggest activity, but all of them suggest sound.

D. Stanza 4 suggests eagerness and action: wished all winter, rush out, hugging the snow.

7. C

A simile is a figure of speech used to compare different things. A simile uses the words *like* or *as*.

A. A metaphor is also a comparison, but it compares through a direct statement; for example, *Harry is a tiger when he's angry*. In this poem, the line "Trees shrug snow from their branches" is a metaphor that directly compares snow-covered trees with people.

B. "A great snow hushes the big sounds of the city." There is no comparison in the sentence. It is a plain description of how falling snow absorbs sound.

C. In the expression "voices ringing in air as clear as an empty glass," the clear air is being compared with an empty glass. The comparison is made using the word *as*; therefore, this is a simile.

D. The sentence "City kids have wished all winter for this morning" does not contain a figure of speech. This is a statement of fact.

8. C

The phrase "Bus-bulls, tires spinning, snort and paw" contains both direct description and metaphor.

A. The image of a bull pawing suggests a lot of action. It does not suggest a sudden stop. Also, when buses stop suddenly, the tires do not spin.

B. Tires spinning are noisy, and "snorting" suggests the roar of a bus engine. However, the main image is of action, not just noise.

C. "Pawing" suggests a lot of movement, but mostly in one place. Along with "snorting" and "tires spinning," the phrase describes buses struggling in the snow.

D. If the buses' tires are spinning, then the buses are not speeding through the snow. They can hardly move.

9. D

There are different moods in this poem. Read carefully to see how the relationship between the snow and the city is described.

A. In the last stanza, the city kids are excited. However, there is no excitement in the other three stanzas.

B. In stanza 1, "The big city is rude to snow," and in stanza 2, "Sometimes… a snowfall captures the city." There is no friendship.

C. Mistrust is not mentioned. Stanza 1 is about rejection. Stanza 2 describes snow capturing the city. In stanza 3, the snow hushes the city. In stanza 4, kids rush outside to hug the snow.

D. According to the poem, the city usually rejects the snow, but occasionally snow captures the city. These are images of conflict. After the capture, there is more struggle and conflict as traffic tries to move. Given the last two stanzas, the relationship between the people and the snow is definitely not one of conflict, but the question asks about the relationship between the city and the snow.

10. B

Only one choice can be backed up with evidence from the poem.

A. In stanza 2, the statement "Sometimes… a snowfall captures the city" suggests that blizzards don't happen often.

B. Stanza 1 is all about the snow not staying: on the branches, the sidewalks, the gutters, and even the ground. The statement "And so the snow melts into slush, pretends that it never was" indicates that the snow usually melts quickly. Also, the fact that the kids have "wished all winter for this morning" implies that this was the only real snow all winter.

C. In stanza 2, police blow their whistles, buses struggle to move, and the snowplows stall. It seems that the city is not ready for heavy snow.

D. There is no mention of damage, and the last two stanzas are peaceful.

THE LIBRARY CARD

11. D

First, be careful to note the words *most likely*. The novel excerpt does not explicitly tell you the answer to this question. You must read carefully and use clues in the story to help you determine the answer.

The introduction to the story gives the strongest clues: "*The librarian did such a good job of promoting the contest that throughout the neighbourhood, television sets were being switched off.*" Given that a contest referred to as "The Great TV Turn-Off" is being promoted by a librarian, it must have something to do with books. This clue helps eliminate alternatives B (television show) and C (broken television).

Both alternatives A (library book) and D (reading challenge) are suitable because a librarian would support reading a library book or taking part in a reading challenge. The excerpt says that the librarian was promoting a contest. A reading challenge would be referred to as a contest, whereas a library book would not. Therefore, the answer is D.

12. D

The word "tombstone" could communicate the idea of eeriness (A), coldness (B), or hardness (C) if it were used in different contexts. In this story, the word "tombstone" is used to communicate the emptiness (D) that Brenda feels while looking at the grey screen of the TV, which is usually flickering with activity.

13. B

Why did Brenda get under the covers and put the pillow under her legs?

A. Brenda's thoughts are completely consumed with television. She seems so addicted to television that simply getting under the covers and putting a pillow under her legs would not help her forget about the TV at all. This would not help her ignore the TV.

B. Brenda was in shock. She remembered from watching TV that to help someone in shock, you should keep the person warm and raise his or her feet. Brenda got under the covers and put the pillow under her legs in order to look after herself in her state of shock.

C. Trying to get some sleep would probably be impossible for Brenda because of the state that she was in. The story describes her as being in shock, upset, and panicked. Trying to get some sleep would probably be the last thing on Brenda's mind at a time like that.

D. Brenda thought about different programs, but this was not the reason she got under the covers and put the pillow under her legs.

14. B

This question asks you why Brenda panicked at 7:25.

A. Brenda is an avid TV watcher, so it is unlikely that she forgot what program was showing. The program that was showing at that time was her favourite; therefore, it was probably all she could think about.

B. Brenda panicked at 7:25 because she had not been able to watch her favourite TV show, *The Dennison Twins*. She had not missed an episode in three years.

C. Brenda went through the experience of not feeling like her room was her own before the panic set in at 7:25.

D. Brenda was keeping very close track of time in this excerpt. Twenty-five minutes had passed up to this point in the story; however, this was not the reason Brenda panicked.

15. B

You know that *Ace Monahan* was showing before 7:00 because line 9 says it was showing on TV "just moments before." Therefore, it is logical to assume that *Ace Monahan* was showing from 6:30 to 7:00. This information eliminates alternatives A and D because both have *The Dennison Twins* scheduled for 6:30.

Alternatives B and C remain. The order of the shows is the same, but the scheduled times are different. You know that *The Dennison Twins* began at 7:00 because "moments before" the TV was turned off at 7:00, *Ace Monahan* had still been on. The final information you need to answer this question is given in lines 39 and 40. These lines tell you that as soon as *The Dennison Twins* is over at 7:30, *Pardon My Petunia* begins. The schedule that correctly shows the times for Brenda's favourite shows is B.

NANCY

16. C

Why does Nancy first speak to the boy?

A. Even though Nancy asks the boy if he can read the sign, she is not really interested in whether or not he can. Her intention in asking the question is to let the boy know that he is not obeying the sign.

B. At no time in this comic strip does Nancy make excuses about the boy's behaviour. She criticizes his behaviour throughout the comic strip.

C. The reason that Nancy speaks to the boy is that he is leaning up against a wall with a sign that reads "No loitering." The boy is loitering; therefore, he is not paying attention to the sign. The boy is standing around where he should not be.

D. The boy is leaning up against the wall wasting time; however, this is not the reason Nancy first speaks to him. If the boy had been leaning on a wall that did not have a sign, Nancy would probably not have spoken to him at all.

17. C

Answer this question by reading the words and studying the cartoonist's depiction of Nancy, including her body language.

A. Nancy's eyes are closed in the second-to-last frame. The boy has not yet said anything to embarrass Nancy, so this is not the correct answer.

B. The cartoonist has drawn Nancy with her finger pointed in three frames: the second, third, and last. Nancy is embarrassed in the last frame when the boy teases her about obeying signs. However, her finger is pointed in more than just this last frame, so this answer is not likely.

C. The boy embarrasses Nancy in the last frame by telling her to obey the sign that says "Don't blow your horn." The last frame is the only frame where Nancy is embarrassed. In this frame, the cartoonist has drawn Nancy with lines over her head to show that she is embarrassed.

D. Nancy's hand is behind her head in the second-to-last frame. The boy has not yet said anything to embarrass Nancy, so this is not the correct answer.

18. A

What is the main idea of the final frame?

Nancy continuously tells the boy that he is doing what he shouldn't be doing according to the signs they pass. In the second-to-last and third-to-last frames, Nancy goes on and on about how she is a model citizen because she obeys all signs. In order to correctly answer this question, you need to know that the phrase "blowing your own horn" is often used when people brag about themselves. The main idea of the final frame is that the boy is telling Nancy that she, in fact, does not follow signs because she is "blowing her own horn" in front of a sign that says "Don't blow your horn." His intention is to tell Nancy not to be boastful.

Answers B, C, and D may be chosen incorrectly if you are unfamiliar with the meaning of the phrase "Don't blow your horn." If the phrase is taken literally, you would think that the boy is telling Nancy to be quiet in front of the sign. This is not the case. He is actually getting Nancy back for having criticized his behaviour as they passed various signs.

THE RICE CAKES

19. A

Answering questions like these can be tricky. The answers are implicit in the story, which means that the answers are not stated: they must be understood from the characters' words and actions.

A. From lines 19 to 25, Ki Jung argues that he should have the last rice cake. His wife's eyes never leave the rice cake, and she never says a word. When Ki Jung exploded in anger, it was because his wife would not give up the rice cake.

B. Ki Jung said that he had lost all his energy, but you know from lines 10 to 15 that he had energy to bang through the gate and shout a question, and enough energy to grab at the first cake and devour it. It was his greed that made him say he is weak.

C. Ki Jung's wife does not argue. She never says a word. Ki Jung says that she will not let him eat the rice cake in peace, but he was angry because she would not give it to him. The best answer is still A.

D. In lines 13 to 14, Ki Jung's stomach is said to be "fairly hollow from hunger," but then he eats two rice cakes. Of course, it is possible that Ki Jung really is feeling hollow, even after two cakes. Yet other parts of the story (lines 1 to 5, 9 and 10, 15, and 36 to 39) show that he is unreasonable about rice cakes. In fact, he is greedy, and the reader doesn't believe what he says.

20. C

The answer to this question is also implicit. You are not told directly why Ki Jung and his wife do not try to stop the thief.

A. Ki Jung and his wife could have spoken at any time. They did not say a word because neither one wanted to speak or move first.

B. They could not have been protecting the rice cakes. There was only one cake left (line 18). As well, Ki Jung and his wife were having a contest to see which one would get to eat the last cake. They were not protecting the cake, they were competing for it.

C. Both of them were determined to not speak or move first, because the last one to move or speak would get to eat the rice cake.

D. They knew he was a thief. They silently watched the man leave with their possessions (lines 36 and 37). Their greed made them stay silent and not move.

21. C

The answer is stated directly in the story; that is, the answer is explicitly given.

A. There is nothing to show that the thief even saw the rice cake. Also, the thief thought that the man and his wife were frozen in terror (lines 33 and 35).

B. You read that the man gathers up whatever he could steal and then leaves. Also, there is nothing to show that the thief even saw the rice cake.

C. The thief thought that the couple were frozen in terror (line 35). This is the reason the thief did not leave.

D. It is clear that the thief knew that the man and his wife were aware of him. As soon as he saw Ki Jung and his wife, he thought that they must have been frozen in terror at the sight of him (lines 33 to 35).

22. D

The answer to this question is implicit in the story.

A. According to line 26, Ki Jung was angry with his wife. He was angry with his wife before the thief comes in, so this cannot be the answer.

B. Ki Jung did not realize that anything had been stolen until the thief was leaving. However, that is the question: why was he so slow to realize that things had been stolen? This response is simply repeating the question in the form of a statement.

C. There is nothing in the story to suggest that Ki Jung thought that only his wife's possessions were stolen; in fact, according to line 36, Ki Jung and his wife both watched as the thief stole some of Ki Jung's possessions.

D. Throughout this story, Ki Jung is portrayed as a greedy man. He thought all day about supper, he was impatient to start eating, he devoured his food greedily, he shouted at his wife, and he invented stories to persuade his wife to give him the last cake. The reason that he took so long to realize what had happened is implicit in all these facts. He was so greedily determined to have the last rice cake that he didn't understand what was happening in front of him.

23. C

When does the main problem begin?

A. By the time that Ki Jung and his wife noticed the thief, the problem that the story is about had already begun.

B. Ki Jung's wife eats faster and catches up to him. As a result, they have eaten the same number of cakes when they have to decide who gets the last cake. At this point, they could agree to be sensible and share. The main problem hasn't started yet.

C. The main problem starts when Ki Jung and his wife will not share the last rice cake. If they had shared the rice cake, they would not have been sitting silently and the thief would not have "decided no one was at home" (line 32).

D. If Ki Jung's neighbour had made six rice cakes, then maybe there would not have been a problem at all. However, should the neighbour be blamed for the greed of Ki Jung and his wife? That doesn't seem fair. This is not the best answer.

TO TOUCH THE MAMMOTH

24. A

What is the meaning of the word "shrill" in line 1 of the story? Use the context around the word to determine its meaning. A trumpeting sound that was *gentle* (B), *distant* (C) or *gradual* (D) could not have "pierced the morning calm." The only logical answer for this question is A. A sharp trumpeting sound would pierce the morning calm.

25. B

Why did Zol set out to touch a mammoth? The answer to this question is not stated explicitly in the story excerpt. Use the clues in the story to figure out the reason that Zol set out to touch a mammoth.

A. Zol is already a member of the Star Dancer tribe. This information is given in the introductory sentence of the story excerpt.

B. The introductory sentence of the story states that Zol is a young member of the tribe and that only one person has ever touched a mammoth. Touching a mammoth must be very rare and dangerous if it has only been accomplished once before. Line 6 tells us that a Star Dancer needs to have courage. Zol wants to be the second person to touch a mammoth to prove that he is courageous.

C. Zol could show that he was able to track mammoths without touching one.

D. Zol could find out where the mammoths were located without touching a mammoth.

26. A

A. Line 16 states that "mammoths had poor eyesight." Sight is the mammoths' weakest sense.

B. The story excerpt does not mention anything about mammoths' sense of taste, so this cannot be the answer.

C. Line 17 states that mammoths have a good sense of smell. This is the reason that Zol must be sure to stand downwind from them.

D. The mammoth touches Zol in the story, but there is no mention about the strength of this sense; therefore, this answer is not the correct choice.

27. B

Why did the young mammoth encounter Zol?

A. It is unlikely that the young mammoth followed Zol because Zol spotted the herd of mammoths in the distance and then moved slowly toward them. If the mammoth had followed Zol, the mammoth would have been behind him.

B. Lines 20 to 21 contain the answer to this question. They say that the "young mammoth had strayed away from the herd." Answer B is another way of saying this. The mammoth wandered near Zol.

C. Zol moved in absolute silence in order to avoid being noticed by the herd of mammoths; therefore, this answer is not the reason the mammoth encountered Zol.

D. Zol could have found somewhere to hide, but the mammoth's presence next to him was very much unexpected. Zol was observing the herd when the mammoth wandered up to his observation point.

28. B

Why are the words "*Do not run!*"in italics in the story? The story says that Zol's heart was beating very quickly in his chest. This happens when someone is very excited or frightened. Zol was sure to be very quiet while observing the mammoths so that he did not scare them off. Ordering (A), shouting (C), and whispering (D) are all sounds that would potentially alarm the mammoth. Zol wants to be very sure not to do this because he is afraid of being injured by the mammoth. The italics emphasize that Zol was thinking these words. The answer is B.

29. B

What does the expression "collapsed like a skin without bones" mean?

A. You know that Zol was not injured by the mammoth because in line 36, he is smiling about his experience. Smiling would not be the expression of a person injured by a mammoth.

B. Zol was definitely frightened by his encounter with the mammoth. You know this because he screamed (line 30) and because when he put his hand over his mouth, he was "wild-eyed with fear" (line 31). When a person is frightened, his or her body is very tense. When the mammoth moved away from Zol without injuring him, Zol's body simply gave out on him as a result of all of the pent-up stress of the experience. The expression "collapsed like a skin without bones" suggests that Zol had been frightened by his encounter and that immediately after, he collapsed with relief.

C. This encounter was very rare. Zol would have been so full of adrenaline that he would not be feeling exhausted, hungry, or thirsty. He would be feeling exhilarated.

D. Zol did not hide after the mammoth lumbered off. He drank from the stream.

MAKING BUTTER

30. D

When does the jar no longer need to be shaken? The answer to this question is stated explicitly in the text.

A. When the cream has become foamy, you still need to continue shaking the jar. The cream is just changing form at this point in the butter-making process.

B. To begin, the cream needs to be taken out of the refrigerator to warm up a little bit. This happens before the cream is put in the jar and the shaking begins.

C. When granules of butter start to form, continue shaking the jar.

D. Instruction 6 says, "When the granules are the size of apple seeds, stop shaking."

31. D

Why are the numbers 1 to 10 used in this passage?

A. The instructions for making butter are clear and fairly simple. The simplicity of the instructions have nothing to do with the numbering. It is very likely that other passages with more difficult instructions would also be numbered.

B. Some, but not all, of the directions tell you how long the step will take. Unless the directions in the number tell you how long the step takes, you do not know. The number does not represent a unit of time such as minutes, hours, etc.

C. The steps are not listed in the order of importance. All steps in a recipe are equally important. Making a recipe without following one of the steps would result in a failed product.

D. The numbers 1 to 10 are used in this passage to ensure that all of the instructions are followed in order. If the instructions were not numbered and a person mixed up the steps, the butter would not turn out as it should.

32. C

Why might salt need to be added to the butter?

A. The passage does not mention how to keep the butter fresh.

B. Adding salt would not make the butter smooth. The passage does not mention how to make the butter smooth.

C. Instruction 9 says, "If you like salty butter, add a little salt." The word "salty" describes a taste; therefore, salt may be added to change the taste of the butter.

D. The section entitled "*Mellow Yellow*" tells how to improve the colour of the butter. Dairies use food colouring to improve the colour of butter.

33. B

What do the underlined words "coalesced" and "coalescing" refer to?

The answer to this question can be found in the "How does it work?" paragraph of the passage. Coalescing occurs when the droplets of butter are "forced together" to "form globules of butter." Butter globules coalesce when they come together. The answer is B.

34. A

Why is the section "*Yellow Mellow*" in a box?

A. This section gives information about butter but not about making butter, which is the topic of the passage. This information about the colour of butter does not tell someone how to make butter; therefore, it is placed on the same page, but in a separate box.

B. This section does not give any explanation about the process of making butter. It provides information about why butter can be different colours.

C. A summary tells the most important points of a passage. This section provides new information; therefore, it is not a summary of the passage.

D. Although this section does share some interesting information, it does not contain the most important information on the page because it does not tell the steps of how to make butter.

THE GREENHORN ON SKIS

35. B

This question is easy if you know the words "tottering," "bumbled," "lurched," and "zipped." If you do not know them, think about the context in which they are used.

A. Is the skier careless? "A day-old colt" (line 9) is not careless, just unsteady. A day-old colt is new to walking. The skier is new to skiing. Also, throughout the poem, the skier is making a great effort. He is not careless.

B. Is the skier unsteady? Yes, he is compared with a colt. The word "tottering" is actually used to describe the colt, not the skier. He is unsteady just as a new colt is unsteady.

C. Is the skier travelling quickly? Not if he is making "erratic starts and stops" (line 14). He also flounders on his back (line 21), then heaves himself up—only to fall down again (line 29).

D. Is the skier barely moving? From line 13 to line 29, the skier is moving a lot, although he is not moving very far from his starting point. The four words and the context in which they are used suggest movement, even if the movement is not very effective.

36. B

To answer this question, it helps to know what is meant by the expression "seeing stars." This old saying refers to seeing spots of light after experiencing a blow to the head. If you do not know the saying, you must use context clues and think through the possible responses.

A. Read lines 1 to 4. It is dawn, so the sun will just be rising. The snow gleams with light like diamonds, so the sun is shining. Can we say the sky is bright? When the sun is just rising, even a cloudless sky cannot be called bright.

B. In line 19, the skier's "feet zipped out ahead of him," and in line 21, "He floundered on his back for a while." This tells us that he fell on his back. We can infer that he hit his head. When the skier is flat on his back, he is looking at the sky. Then, without knowing about seeing stars, you can make another inference, or conclusion, based on evidence. "His sky" is what he sees. "Stars" are what he sees when he has hit his head.

C. Yes, the snow sparkled like diamonds (line 2). However, the quotation refers to the skier's sky, not in the snow.

D. Did the skier lie on the snow until night? No. According to lines 23 to 24, he heaved himself up.

37. C

The question is really asking for the meaning of "greenhorn." The word is used three times in the 32 lines, but the whole poem is about the greenhorn skier. The whole poem is the context.

A. There is no way of telling if the skier is unathletic. He might be very good at many other sports. Is he weak? Again, there is no way to tell. You only know that he is unsteady on the snow.

B. The skier tries really hard and doesn't let his falls upset him. When he falls for the last time in line 29, he laughs and makes a joke out of it. This greenhorn is not scared of new things.

C. The skier's struggles suggest that he has never been on skis before. A greenhorn is someone who is new to something. He has little or no experience.

D. The writer does make the skier's clothes seem funny. His toque "squeezed his head" (line 6), so the toque must be too small for him. The pom-pom on his white toque "is like a cherry ripe and red" (line 8). The description is meant to seem ridiculous. However, you cannot tell about the skier's taste in clothes. Maybe he is wearing borrowed clothes.

38. C

To understand the purpose of the poem, you must think about the whole poem. Notice that the question does not ask about the main purpose; this omission indicates that there is only one possible answer.

A. To *convince* means to make someone certain of something or to persuade someone to do something. There is nothing in this poem that would change your thinking about something. This poem is not intended to convince.

B. To *inform* means to give information or knowledge. The poem tells about a greenhorn's first attempt at skiing. Can you call that information or knowledge? No. There is no attempt to inform.

C. To *amuse* means to make someone laugh. Everything in this poem is light-hearted and amusing. The only purpose of this poem is to amuse.

D. To *warn* means to tell someone about something that could cause injury or some other kind of harm. It is possible to be hurt by suddenly doing the splits (line 32). However, the skier laughs about it. Readers are also meant to laugh. This poem does not warn.

STORY WITHOUT WORDS

39. A

This question is answered by reading carefully.

A. Line 9: "Ballet started in Italy about 500 years ago." This is the correct answer. The other countries are mentioned in the order in which ballet spread to them. Also notice the words used to organize the third and fourth paragraphs. These words show the order: "started," "became," "also became."

B. Line 9: "It became popular in France."

C. Line 15: "Ballet also became popular in the Soviet Union."

D. The United States is not mentioned in this article.

40. A

Be careful to note the words *most likely*. There is no explicit statement that tells why ballet terms are French.

A. Ballet first became popular in France. "All the steps... received French names." We can infer that no one ever felt it was necessary to change the names.

B. Ballet was not a traditional dance in France. It was invented in Italy and became popular as a special form of entertainment for the king of France (lines 9 to 10).

C. The French names for ballet terms are now used in every country (line 11), but this does not mean that many people in every country understand French.

D. Music is not written in words, but in musical notes. Classical composers generally did not write words for their compositions, but those who did used a variety of languages. The passage does not refer to this.

41. A

Be careful with this kind of question! You might think that this question could be answered by looking only at the illustration. However, there is one important fact that you need to know before looking at the picture.

A. The dancers' arms, legs, and feet are in different positions in each of the five pictures. In line 7, we learn that there are five basic positions in ballet. The illustration, which is labelled "Basic Positions," obviously shows these five basic, unique positions.

B. There is nothing in the picture or the text to suggest that only males perform positions 2 and 4. The males and females in the illustrations are demonstrating different steps.

C. Many people have seen ballet on the stage or on television. Many people know that dancers do move gracefully from one position to the next. However, there is nothing in the illustration or text that states this fact.

D. The illustrations show arms, legs, and feet carefully place in each position. There is nothing to suggest that arms are more important than anything else.

42. D

All of the responses to this question are true statements. However, only one explains why "Story Without Words" is a good title.

A. Classical music usually has no words. In ballet, the story is told through dance, not music (line 1).

B. People who speak different languages can dance ballet, but ballet does not require words. The dancers' languages are unimportant.

C. Ballet is a special form of entertainment, but so is opera, which is full of words.

D. Ballet dancers communicate through movement to tell "a story without words." (line 1).

THE COMICS

43. A

You must recognize the formats (or the way that things are presented or arranged) of interviews, outlines, reports, and plays.

A. The Qs and As show that this is an interview. The cartoonist is answering questions.

B. The format looks a little like an outline format, although outlines often have numbering or lettering through which the main points are organized. An outline could be written in question and answer format. However, an outline is a plan of the main points in a larger project, so this is not an outline.

C. In a way, this interview is a report. The interviewer is reporting on Lynn Johnston. However, the format of this "report" is the format of an interview.

D. A play printed in a book will look a little like this interview, except that each paragraph would begin with the character's name.

44. B

The important thing to understand is the meaning of RECORD. This word is a reference to the "record" button on a video or tape recorder. Lynn Johnston is always "recording" what she hears or sees. What if you don't understand her special use of the word? After all, a good dictionary has a number of different meanings for the word "record." The most likely place to find information that will help you answer the question is in the context of the quotation.

A. The words "write and rewrite" are found in lines 9 and 10. In these lines, she is talking about working on the writing for each strip.

B. Line 5 contains the full sentence with the words "I'm on RECORD all the time, getting ideas." The end of the sentence makes it clear that Lynn Johnston is talking about getting ideas. She is referring to pressing the RECORD button on a tape or video recording machine and leaving it on. She records everything to use in her cartoon strip.

C. Lynn Johnston talks about working to meet deadlines in her fourth response. Nothing about deadlines matches any of the meanings of "RECORD."

D. In her last response, Johnston talks about cartoonists developing style, but this is not related to her quotations about being "on RECORD."

45. A

To determine why Lynn Johnston wears a cotton glove, you must make an inference based on what she says.

A. In her third response, Lynn Johnston says that her fingers perspire (or sweat) a lot. She wears cotton gloves to keep her drawings clean. Sweaty fingers will make a pencil drawing dirty by smudging it. Lynn Johnston wears cotton gloves to avoid smudging her work.

B. Lynn Johnston says that if she makes a mistake (her third response), she covers the mistake with animation paint. She doesn't say anything about avoiding mistakes.

C. Cold hands are not mentioned anywhere.

D. We can infer that the cotton glove that keeps Lynn Johnston's drawing clean will also keep her hand clean. However, what would be an artist's main concern? The drawing, of course.

46. B

Do you know what writer's block is? If you do, then cartoonist's block will be no problem. Otherwise, you will need to use the context to see what Lynn Johnston says about cartoonist's block.

A. Lines 20 to 22 are about planning ahead. People sometimes speak of "blocks of time" when they are planning, but Lynn Johnston only speaks of writing each strip six weeks ahead of time (line 20).

B. The interviewer's fifth question asks if there is such a thing as cartoonist's block. In the next line, Lynn Johnston replies that there are "dry times" when she has no ideas. That means that she is agreeing with the interviewer. The dry times when she has no ideas are the times when she has cartoonist's block.

C. The only time sleep is mentioned is in line 26. Lynn Johnston is not unable to sleep. Sometimes she sleeps when she has no ideas. "Sleep can be part of the creative process" (lines 26 to 27). Sleeping is not about cartoonist's block. It is one way that Lynn Johnston takes care of cartoonist's block.

D. Sometimes Lynn Johnson reads "something funny to get in a good mood" (line 26). She does this when she has no ideas. Reading something funny is not cartoonist's block. It is one method that Lynn Johnston uses to take care of cartoonist's block.

47. D

Attitude is a general feeling or opinion about something. This question is about attitude and being successful. All of the responses are statements made by Lynn Johnston. One of the responses is about attitude and success.

A. "I do both the writing and the drawing" is a statement of fact. There nothing here about what Lynn Johnston feels or thinks.

B. "Sleep can be part of the creative process" is a statement of opinion or advice about how to get over cartoonist's block, not about attitude or success.

C. "Copying isn't bad unless you say someone else's work is yours" is part of Lynn Johnston's advice about becoming a comic-strip artist. The statement is part of her advice about practising. It is not about attitude. Lynn Johnston is saying that young people can practise by copying the work of experts.

D. "And never say 'I'm good,' say 'I could be better'" is a statement about a cartoonist's attitude toward work. Lynn Johnston is saying that it is important to always have the attitude that good work can be improved.

BETTER OR WORSE CARTOON

48. A

There are two steps to answering this question. The first step is to study the first frame of the comic strip. In the first frame, Elizabeth looks sad. A tear runs down her cheek. The second step is to think about the meanings of the words in the four alternatives.

A. Sulking: being silent and withdrawn in resentment or protest. In the first frame, Elizabeth is silent. She seems sad and upset. There is a tear running down her cheek. Is she resentful or protesting? It is hard to say, but we can say that she is silent, withdrawn, and upset, which makes *sulking* the closest word to *moping*.

B. Whining: complaining childishly, often in an annoying, high-pitched voice. In the picture, Elizabeth is silent. She cannot be whining.

C. Complaining: expressing pain, dissatisfaction, or resentment. Again, Elizabeth is silent. She is not expressing anything.

D. Daydreaming: letting the mind wander in distracting—usually pleasant—thoughts. Elizabeth is sad about something. Her thoughts are not pleasant. She does not look as though she is letting her thoughts wander. She is not daydreaming.

49. D

In the third frame, Elizabeth's eyes are wide open and her mouth is down a little on one side. Her expression shows uncertainty.

A. Elizabeth is uncertain. She cannot be both uncertain and disbelieving. If she does not believe, then she would not be uncertain. Rather, she would be certain that she does not believe her father.

B. It might be possible to be uncertain and not want to listen. Look at the next frame. Elizabeth's "Oh" shows that she has heard her father and that she now has different feelings. It is possible that Elizabeth does not want to listen, but it is not the best answer.

C. Elizabeth's expression in the first frame shows that she is really upset about her haircut. Her expression in the third frame is completely different. This response cannot be the answer.

D. Elizabeth's uncertain expression should be looked at together with the next frame in which she says "Oh." Elizabeth is considering her problem in a new way.

50. A

Three of the responses are related. That is why the word **main** is bolded.

A. Look at the third frame. Elizabeth's father lists really bad problems. Then, in the last frame, he says, "And you have problem hair." He is comparing Elizabeth's problem with a list of serious problems. He is showing her that her problem is really small. The main idea is to keep our problems in perspective. To keep things in perspective means to see small problems as they really are.

B. Maybe you should never be upset by your problems. Maybe you should be upset sometimes. Either way, the cartoon says nothing about it.

C. To be more concerned about others than ourselves means to put other people's concerns first. Putting other people first is often a good idea. This response is related to the main idea, but it doesn't fit as well as alternative A.

D. Elizabeth's father is just comparing Elizabeth's hair problem with real problems. He wants Elizabeth to realize that her problem is quite small. He is not talking about knowing what is happening in the world.

Answers and Solutions
2001 Provincial Achievement Test

1. *	**11. ***	**21. A**	**31. ***	**41. C**
2. *	**12. ***	**22. D**	**32. ***	**42. D**
3. *	**13. ***	**23. B**	**33. ***	**43. D**
4. *	**14. ***	**24. ***	**34. ***	**44. D**
5. *	**15. ***	**25. ***	**35. C**	**45. A**
6. B	**16. C**	**26. ***	**36. A**	**46. A**
7. C	**17. D**	**27. ***	**37. D**	**47. A**
8. B	**18. D**	**28. ***	**38. D**	**48. ***
9. A	**19. C**	**29. ***	**39. B**	**49. ***
10. D	**20. D**	**30. ***	**40. B**	**50. ***

* *See answers and solutions from the 2000 Provincial Achievement Test.*

THE INSIDE STORY OF A WASPS' NEST

The article excerpt THE INSIDE STORY OF A WASPS' NEST and questions 1 to 5 are not reprinted here as they are a repeat of the 2000 Provincial Achievement Test included in this resource.

THE ATTIC

6. B

What does the word "shrouds" refer to in the poem?

Use the context of this word to determine its meaning. Lines 1 and 3 give clues to the meaning of this word. The words "curtains gray" are in line 1, and line 3 says, "Wrap windows with." These clues help to eliminate the answers (A), (C), and (D). A window cannot be wrapped in the sky (A) or in a secret place (D). A poet could say that a window with sun beaming on it was wrapped in sunlight (C), but it would be bright not "gray." In this poem, the word "shrouds" refers to a covering.

7. C

Note that the word *main* is bolded. This means that there is one best answer for this question.

A. Although the words "Right here" do mark the end of every sentence in this poem, a period does, too. Therefore, this is not the main purpose of these words.

B. The words "Right here" do communicate a satisfactory ending, but this is not the poet's main purpose. The poet could have used other words to do this.

C. The poet uses the words "Right here" to emphasize the importance of the setting. The setting of the poem is the attic, which is also the title of the poem.

D. The words "Right here" do provide a rhyme for the last word of each stanza, but this is not the poet's **main** purpose for using this phrase. The poet could have found many other words to provide a rhyme.

8. B

Note the word *mainly* is bolded. This means that the poet may think of the attic in different ways, but there is one best answer.

A. The poet may think of the attic as a place to rest because of the privacy, familiar surroundings, and memories that the attic holds, but the question asks how the poet *mainly* thinks of the attic.

B. The mood of the poem is very light. The poet thinks of the attic as a very special place. A good clue is that the phrase "This is my place to dream" repeats throughout the poem.

C. Although there are many things in the attic, it is not described as a cluttered and messy place; in fact, line 13 "Where walls are hung" indicates at least some neatness.

D. In the last stanza, the narrator says that in the future, certain things will recall him or her to the attic in order "to dream." There is nothing dark or frightening about this image. In line 30, the word "dark" describes a pane of glass in a way that will remind the narrator fondly of the attic.

9. A

Line 14 can be used to determine the meaning of this phrase. Line 14 tells us that it is grandpa's gear that is hanging on the walls; therefore, this phrase means that the walls are lined with objects. The other answers are not logical. They take the meaning of this phrase literally as if the walls are actually being held up by ropes (B), broken down (C), or tied together (D).

10. D

Line 26 provides a clue to the answer to this question. It talks about a time when the narrator will be "far away."

A. One would not expect the narrator to visit the attic *often* when she is older if she is far away. Living far away would make it difficult to visit the attic very often.

B. Given the detail in the poem, the narrator has already looked carefully in the attic. She will not have to wait until she is older to do so.

C. This attic is very special to her; therefore, she probably would not compare this attic to other places.

D. When a place is very special to a person, it is common to be reminded of that place when something like a smell or object triggers a memory. The narrator expects that when she is older, she will sometimes be reminded of the attic.

THE LIBRARY CARD

The story excerpt THE LIBRARY CARD and questions 11 to 15 are not reprinted here as they are a repeat of the 2000 Provincial Achievement Test included in this resource.

HÄGAR THE HORRIBLE

16. C

How do the words "DECISIONS, DECISIONS, DECISIONS!" in frame 2 make the reader feel?

A. The reader does not yet have any reason to be disappointed with the Viking. There is no context on which to base this feeling; therefore, this is not the correct answer.

B. The Viking has not yet done anything that has potential to make the reader become angry.

C. Everyone has to make some hard decisions in life. It is difficult to be the person who has to make a lot of decisions. People would be sympathetic to someone faced with making "DECISIONS, DECISIONS, DECISIONS!" These words are used in order to make the reader sympathize with the Viking.

D. Frame 2 is only the second frame in the comic strip. At this point, humour is not yet quite established, so the words "DECISIONS, DECISIONS, DECISIONS!" are not used in order to make the reader laugh at the Viking.

17. D

To determine the meaning of the Viking's expression, read the text of the comic strip.

A. The Viking's expression in frame 4 could be considered hesitation, but the text does not support this feeling. There is nothing in the comic text that would lead one to believe that the Viking is feeling hesitation—until asked about what he would like for breakfast.

B. The expression on the Viking's face may be one of confusion; however, the text accompanying the expression does not support this interpretation. He is definitely not confused about whose job it is to make the decisions. This is shown by the word "I" being written in bold to emphasize the word.

C. The Viking's expression is probably not one of excitement. He says that the job is stressful and there are tough decisions to be made. His comments do not lead one to believe that his expression is one of excitement.

D. The Viking is taking his job very seriously and his expression matches this. He continues to talk about the many important decisions he needs to make. The bolded "I" in frame 4 shows that he is taking the responsibility seriously; therefore, his expression is one of seriousness.

18. D

The only logical answer is the comment, "Do you want bacon and eggs or pancakes for breakfast?" The other comments all help build up to the humour in the comment about breakfast. This comment is humorous because the Viking went on and on about what a tough job he has and how he is in charge of making such big, important decisions. When he is asked a simple question about his breakfast preference, he considers it as one of the tough questions he was anticipating. The answer to this question is (D).

I SURVIVED THE TITANIC

19. C

A. The *Titanic* was sinking. Captain Smith would not have time to keep the passengers informed. He would be too busy telling his crew what needed to be done.

B. The captain ordered the radio operator to send messages to other ships asking for help. The captain did not send the message to nearby ships himself.

C. Line 6 contains the phrase "Captain Smith fired orders." The sentence immediately following says that radio operators were working. It is logical to think that the radio operators, as members of the crew, are doing what Captain Smith had ordered. The phrase means that Captain Smith gave the crew jobs to do.

D. Line 29 says "the crew fired distress rockets." Captain Smith did not set off emergency flares, the crew did; therefore, this answer is not correct.

20. D

What was Mrs. Becker awakened by?

A. Line 11 says that "Some passengers had been awakened by a slight jolt." Mrs. Becker was not one of the passengers awakened in this manner.

B. Mrs. Becker heard a pounding noise *after* she was awakened by the stopping of the engines.

C. Lines 9 to 10 say that "Stewards started knocking on cabin doors." However, Mrs. Becker's door was never knocked on.

D. The answer to this question is found explicitly in lines 17 to 18: " 'when she was awakened by the engines stopping.' "

21. A

How was Ruth **mainly** feeling as the *Titanic* was sinking?

A. In line 25, Ruth says that she "was only excited."

B. Ruth witnessed other people who were weeping and very frightened. Observing these people and knowing the seriousness of the situation would not lead her to feel amused.

C. Ruth was too excited to feel perturbed about the situation. Her excitement busied her thoughts, so that she did not think of things that may have perturbed her such as the lack of lifeboats.

D. In lines 24 to 25, Ruth says, " 'But I was never scared.' " The word *scared* is synonymous with frightened; therefore, this is not the correct answer.

22. D

What sense does the sentence "The only hope for the others was help from another ship" create?

This sentence does not create a sense of mystery (A). Mystery means there is something unknown. It was a known fact that if another ship did not help, many people would perish.

There may have been suspense (B) in wondering if another ship would be able to help and frustration (C) with relying on the unknown, but this sentence reflects desperation. The words "only hope" create a sense of desperation (D). Without help from another ship, many people would die.

23. B

Why did people shout to stop lowering lifeboat #15?

A. Ruth was aboard lifeboat #13 at this time. Her boat was beneath the lifeboat that was being lowered.

B. Line 37 tells us that the people were shouting because Ruth's boat was "directly beneath the next lifeboat, #15, being lowered." The people were trying to get the crew to stop lowering lifeboat #15 because it was about to crush the people beneath it in lifeboat #13.

C. Lifeboat #15 was probably 50 feet from the water because it was just being lowered; however, this is not the reason the people were shouting.

D. According to line 36, water was spewing from the Titanic, but this is not the reason the people were shouting.

TO TOUCH THE MAMMOTH

The story excerpt TO TOUCH THE MAMMOTH and questions 24 to 29 are not reprinted here as they are a repeat of the 2000 Provincial Achievement Test included in this resource.

MAKING BUTTER

The article excerpt MAKING BUTTER and questions 30 to 34 are not reprinted here as they are a repeat of the 2000 Provincial Achievement Test included in this resource.

NO ONE HEARD HIM CALL

35. C

What are the sentences "There was no moon. There were no stars" used to develop?

A. These sentences do not give any information about the character in order to further develop what the reader knows of the little boy.

B. A mysterious event could happen in this type of setting, but in the context of this poem, these sentences do not develop any sense of mystery.

C. The setting is where the poem takes place. The setting encompasses all details that help create an image in the reader's mind of where the events are happening. These lines help develop the setting because they let the reader know that it is very dark outside without a moon or stars; therefore, the image created is one of darkness. The poem takes place outside in the dark of the night.

D. The plot of a story or poem consists of the main events. These sentences do not help further develop the plot.

36. A

Note the word "most" is bolded in this question. This means that the boy may feel anxious about more than one thing, but you need to choose the reason he was **most** anxious.

A. The boy went by himself to the woodshed in the dark. You know that he is very anxious about being in the dark alone because the poem tells us that he ran the "whole dark way" there and hurried back. He is most anxious about being alone in the dark.

B. The boy was anxious when he was running around outside in the dark because he does not like being alone in the dark; however, the fact that he was running is not the reason that he is most anxious.

C. The poem does not mention the boy being anxious about losing his way or getting lost in the dark. He made his way to the woodshed and back to the house. He appears to be very familiar with the path from the house to the woodshed.

D. The porch light being out contributed to the boy's anxiety, but the reason it made him anxious was that he was alone in the dark.

37. D

A. The word "Still" is used to show that the boy's efforts to be noticed were unsuccessful. The boy's sense of hope had probably diminished.

B. The entire second half of the poem may make the reader feel sorry for the boy because he cannot get in, but this sentence alone does not establish a sense of regret.

C. A sense of danger is not established with this sentence. Nothing in the poem would lead the reader to believe the boy is in danger.

D. The sentence "Still no one came at all" creates a sense of suspense. The reader is unsure if someone will let the boy inside.

38. D

Why does the woman in the poem say, " 'My goodness, is that you?' "

A. The woman would not say " 'My goodness, is that you?' " if the boy had injured himself and she was upset about it.

B. When the woman opened the door, the light from inside streamed out into the darkness; therefore, she would have been able to see the boy.

C. The reader assumes that the woman who opens the door is the boy's mother. A mother would not be annoyed that her son was pounding on the door if he was locked out in the darkness.

D. The woman would be surprised that the boy was outside by himself in the dark because she probably knew that he was afraid of the dark and assumed that he was already in the house.

WHY DOES POPCORN POP?

39. B

What are the questions at the beginning of the experiment intended to do?

A. There is no opportunity for the reader to reply to the questions; therefore, the questions are not an invitation to reply.

B. The logical answer to this question is (B). The questions at the beginning of the experiment introduce the topic. A topic sentence or sentences are written in order to interest the reader so that he or she continues to read. These questions are intended to cause the reader to become interested in the topic.

C. The questions are not intended to be answered and used to determine what the reader knows. The experiment is already laid out. The reader's knowledge does not affect this experiment in any way.

D. The questions make the reader think about making popcorn. They do not encourage the reader to eat popcorn.

40. B

What do the italicized words "*popping corn*" indicate?

A. The correct pronunciation of the words "popping corn" would be shown by breaking down the word into smaller sound groups. A person could look at the words written in that form and be able to pronounce them.

B. People say popcorn instead of the proper name "*popping corn.*" "*Popping corn*" is italicized to show the proper term for what many people call popcorn.

C. An abbreviation is the short form of a word. Abbreviations usually end with a period. An example of an abbreviation is "Dr." for "doctor."

D. If "*popping corn*" were a brand name, it would be a proper noun. Proper nouns are capitalized (Popping Corn).

41. C

What is the purpose of using a colander in Procedure 2?

A. A colander is a plastic or metal bowl with holes in it. Putting the kernels in a bowl like this would not prevent them from drying out.

B. Kernels need to be heated in order to pop. A colander is not a source of heat, so its purpose is not to hold the kernels while they are popping.

C. The unpopped popcorn is placed in water in Procedure 2. The second sentence in Procedure 2 says to "drain the popcorn in a colander." The purpose of a colander is to hold the kernels while the water drains out.

D. Colanders have tiny holes in them in order to allow water to flow through while keeping the particles in. A colander could not be used to soak kernels because the water escapes through the holes. It cannot hold water for the kernels to soak in.

42. D

Which of the charts shown summarizes the results of this experiment?

This information can be found directly in the experiment. Pay close attention to key words. Table D summarizes the results of this experiment correctly.

The sentence that starts in line 26 provides the correct information to fill in the "**soaked**" condition of the popcorn. It says, "The popcorn that was soaked in water made the **biggest** kernels of popped popcorn as well as the **largest** amount of popcorn." The word *largest* also means **most**.

The sentence that starts in line 30 provides the correct information to fill in the "**dried**" condition of the popcorn. It says, "The dried popcorn kernels made **smaller** kernels of popped popcorn and were more likely to be duds (unpopped kernels)." If they were likely to be duds, this means that they produced the **least** amount of popcorn.

The second sentence that starts in line 32 provides the correct information to fill in the "**left in bag**" condition of the popcorn. It says, "The popcorn that was left in a plastic bag made **medium**-sized kernels of popped popcorn and an **average** amount."

FIGHTING FIT

43. D

Why must a longship have a strong keel?

A. This article excerpt does not mention anything about the keel allowing the longship to land on rocky beaches.

B. It is likely that all the parts of a longship would need to be strong for it to sail in rough seas, but the article excerpt does not mention this.

C. Having a strong keel has nothing to do with supporting a huge sail. The longship must have a strong mast in order to support a huge sail.

D. The first sentence in the section numbered 1 tells you that the keel is the backbone of the boat and that it supports all the other parts. This is another way of saying that the keel holds the longship together.

44. D

A. The ability to quickly raise and lower the mast does not make the longship fast. It allows the crew to "switch from sail to oar at a moment's notice."

B. The deck is flat and kept free of obstacles because the longship is used for fighting. This has nothing to do with the speed of the longship.

C. The crew may be ready to row in an instant, but being ready is not what makes the longship fast.

D. The last paragraph in the section numbered 2 contains the answer to this question. The reason that a longship is extremely fast is that "Each plank of the hull is cut as thinly as possible," which makes a longship "incredibly light." A light ship is a fast ship.

45. A

The article is numbered in sections to show the order in which the parts are assembled. Number 5 is the exception; it discusses how spectacular the longships are. To answer this question, follow the numbers of the article.

Section 1 – keel

Section 2 – hull

Section 3 – deck

Section 4 – mast

The order in which the parts of the Viking longship are assembled is: keel, hull, deck, and mast. The answer is (A).

46. A

Why are the Viking longships "envied throughout Europe"?

A. The Vikings want ships that would benefit them when fighting and sailing. The longships are fast, can travel in shallow water, and can sail in storms. These are the reasons that they are "envied throughout Europe."

B. Longships do have flat decks and backbones, but they are not "envied throughout Europe" for their structure. They are envied for their abilities to help the Vikings sail and fight.

C. Longships have tall masts and are fast, but they are not made from a single tree. If you chose this answer, you misread the information. You are told that it takes a single straight tree to build the keel and a single tree trunk to build the mast. This tells you that the longship already requires two trees. The deck and hull also require planks of wood.

D. Longships can travel in shallow water, but they are probably very expensive to make. The article excerpt does not say outright that the longship is expensive, but it gives some clues. The keel is made from the "very best-quality oak." The best-quality oak would cost more than standard-quality oak. It would also take a lot of time and work to cut the hull planks thinly, and to construct the rest of the boat. Paying skilled workers the time it takes to make a longship would make the boat expensive to build.

47. A

An opinion is a statement that expresses what an individual thinks. An opinion is not a statement of fact or a truth that can be proven.

A. The statement "longships are without a doubt the finest fighting ships" is an opinion. A master boatbuilder states this opinion in the Viking news. The reason for stating this is that the boatbuilder believes he builds the best longships.

B. At first glance, this statement may appear to be an opinion, but it is not. The boatbuilder is speaking about what he will do, not what he thinks. The boatbuilder is stating that he will only use the very best-quality oak. He is not giving his opinion about anything.

C. This statement is factual. The longship does not have any benches. A person can see that this statement is true.

D. This statement is factual. If a mast is not tall enough, it will not support a huge sail.

NANCY

The NANCY cartoon and questions 48 to 50 are not reprinted here as they are a repeat of the 2000 Provincial Achievement Test included in this resource.

NOTES

CREDITS

The publishers wish to thank all those who assisted in the creation of this publication.

Examination questions from the 2000 and 2001 Provincial Achievement Tests have been reproduced with the permission of Alberta Education. Some of the original graphics and materials used in the provincial examinations have been adapted, modified, deleted, or replaced in this publication.

Efforts have been made to provide proper acknowledgment of the original sources and to comply with copyright law. However, some attempts to establish original copyright ownership may have been unsuccessful. If copyright ownership can be identified, please notify Castle Rock Research Corporation so that appropriate corrective action can be taken.

Reading Comprehension Strategies

"Because It Was There" excerpt from *Natural Wonders of the World: Mount Everest*

"Mysterious Black Holes" excerpt from *Explore! A Book of Science*, (Addison Wesley)

Poem *Winter Worries* by Jane W. Krows

Poem *Song of the Pop Bottlers* by Morris Bishop

Poem *My Nose*, by Dorothy Aldis

Cartoon *Barkeater Lake*: © Corey Pandolph/Dist. by United Feature Syndicate, Inc..

2000 Provincial Achievement Test

Illustration from *Where the Forest Meets the Sea* by Jeannie Baker (Scholastic Inc., 1987).

Photograph from *What on Earth is a Capybara?* by Edward R. Ricciuti (Blackbirch Press, Inc., 1995).

"The Inside Story of a Wasps' Nest" from *OWL'S Summer Fun* edited by Laima Dingwall and Annabel Slaight (Greey de Pencier Books, 1984).

"Blizzard" from *Flashlight and Other Poems* by Judith Thurman. Copyright © 1976 Judith Thurman.

Jerry Spinelli. From *The Library Card.* Published by Scholastic Press, a division of Scholastic Inc. Copyright © 1997 by Jerry Spinelli.

Cartoon by Ernie Bushmiller. *Nancy*: © United Feature Syndicate, Inc.

C. Nordhielm Wooldridge. From "The Rice Cakes" as found in *Highlights for Children*, vol. 45, no. 8, September 1990. © 1990.

Patricia Nikolina Clark. From "To Touch the Mammoth" as found in *Highlights for Children*, vol. 52, no. 1, January 1997. Copyright © 1997 by Highlights for Children, Inc., Columbus, Ohio.

"Making Butter" excerpt from *The Jumbo Book of Science* by the Ontario Science Centre with illustrations by Linda Hendry, Pat Cupples, and Tina Holdcroft. Text copyright © 1994 The Ontario Science Centre.

Myra Stilborn. "The Greenhorn on Skis" from *Canadian Children's Annual*, no. 11, 1985.

Illustration by Annalies Davis for "The Greenhorn on Skis" from *Canadian Children's Annual*, no. 11, 1985.

Marcia L. Kaye. From "Story without Words" as found in *Karen Kain* (Fitzhenry & Whiteside Ltd., 1989).

Linda Granfield. From "The Comics" as found in *Extra! Extra!: the who, what, where, when and why of newspapers* (Kids Can Press Ltd., Toronto, 1993). © Linda Granfield.

FOR BETTER OR FOR WORSE © (1994) Lynn Johnston Productions. Dist. By Universal Press Syndicate. Reprinted with permission. All rights reserved.

2001 Provincial Achievement Test

Jane Yolen. "The Attic" from *Cricket*, vol. 22, no. 1, September 1994, edited by Marianne Carus.

Cartoon by Chris Browne. "Hägar the Horrible" © King Features Syndicate

Jennifer A. Kirkpatrick. From "I Survived the Titanic" as found in *National Geographic World*, no. 251, July 1996.

Dorothy Aldis. "No One Heard Him Call" from *Talking Like the Rain* edited by X.J. Kennedy and Dorothy M. Kennedy [Little, Brown & Company (Canada) Limited, 1992].

Illustration by Jane Dyer. For "No One Heard Him Call" from *Talking Like the Rain* edited by X.J. Kennedy and Dorothy M. Kennedy [Little, Brown & Company (Canada) Limited, 1992].

From "Why Does Popcorn Pop?" adapted from *The Jumbo Book of Science* by the Ontario Science Centre with illustrations by Linda Hendry, Pat Cupples, and Tina Holdcroft. Text copyright © 1994 The Ontario Science Centre.

Rachel Wright. From "Shipping News: Fighting Fit" as found in *The Viking News: The Greatest Newspaper in Civilization* (Candlewick Press, 1998).

Illustrations by Christian Hook. From "Shipping News: Fighting Fit" as found in *The Viking News: The Greatest Newspaper in Civilization* by Rachel Wright (Candlewick Press, 1998).

ORDERING INFORMATION

All School Orders

School Authorities are eligible to purchase these resources by applying the Learning Resource Credit Allocation (LRCA – 25% school discount) on their purchase through the Learning Resources Centre (LRC). Call LRC for details.

***THE KEY** Study Guides* are specifically designed to assist students in preparing for unit tests, final exams, and provincial examinations.

***KEY** Study Guides* – $29.95 each plus G.S.T.

SENIOR HIGH		JUNIOR HIGH	ELEMENTARY
Biology 30	Biology 20	Language Arts 9	Language Arts 6
Chemistry 30	Chemistry 20	Math 9	Math 6
English 30-1	English 20-1	Science 9	Science 6
English 30-2	Math 20 (Pure)	Social Studies 9	Social Studies 6
Math 30 (Pure)	Physics 20	Math 8	Math 4
Math 30 (Applied)	Social Studies 20	Math 7	Language Arts 3
Physics 30	English 10-1		Math 3
Social Studies 30	Math 10 (Pure)		
Social Studies 33	Science 10		
	Social Studies 10		

Student Notes and Problems (SNAP) Workbooks contain complete explanations of curriculum concepts, examples, and exercise questions.

SNAP Workbooks – $29.95 each plus G.S.T.

SENIOR HIGH		JUNIOR HIGH	ELEMENTARY
Chemistry 30	Chemistry 20	Math 9	Math 6
Math 30 Pure	Math 20 Pure	Science 9	Math 5
Math 30 Applied	Math 20 Applied	Math 8	Math 4
Math 31	Physics 20	Math 7	Math 3
Physics 30	Math 10 Pure		
	Math 10 Applied		
	Science 10		

Visit our website for a "tour" of resource content and features at
www.castlerockresearch.com

Castle Rock Research Corp

#2340, 10180 – 101 Street
Edmonton, AB Canada T5J 3S4
e-mail: learn@castlerockresearch.com

Phone: 780.448.9619
Toll-free: 1.800.840.6224
Fax: 780.426.3917

2006 (3)

THE KEY	QUANTITY
Biology 30	
Chemistry 30	
English 30-1	
English 30-2	
Math30 (Pure)	
Math 30 (Applied)	
Physics 30	
Social Studies 30	
Social Studies 33	
Biology 20	
Chemistry 20	
English 20-1	
Math 20 (Pure)	
Physics 20	
Social Studies 20	
English 10-1	
Math 10 (Pure)	
Science 10	
Social Studies 10	
Language Arts 9	
Math 9	
Science 9	
Social Studies 9	
Math 8	
Math 7	
Language Arts 6	
Math 6	
Science 6	
Social Studies 6	
Math 4	
Math 3	
Language Arts 3	

SNAP WORKBOOKS Notes and Problems/ Student Notes and Problems	QUANTITY Workbooks	Solutions Manuals
Chemistry 30		
Chemistry 20		
Physics 30		
Physics 20		
Math 30 Pure		
Math 30 Applied		
Math 31		
Math 20 Pure		
Math 20 Applied		
Math 10 Pure		
Math 10 Applied		
Science 10		
Science 9		
Math 9		
Math 8		
Math 7		
Math 6		
Math 5		
Math 4		
Math 3		

TOTALS

KEYS	
WORKBOOKS	
SOLUTION MANUALS	

Learning Resources Centre

Castle Rock Research is pleased to announce an exclusive distribution arrangement with the Learning Resources Centre (LRC). Under this agreement, schools can now place all their orders with LRC for order fulfillment. As well, these resources are eligible for applying the Learning Resource Credit Allocation (LRCA) which gives schools a 25% discount off LRC's selling price. Call LRC for details.

Orders may be placed with LRC by
telephone: (780) 427-5775,
fax: (780) 422-9750,
internet: www.lrc.learning.gov.ab.ca
or mail: 12360 - 142 Street NW
Edmonton, AB T5L 4X9.

Learning Resources Centre

PAYMENT AND SHIPPING INFORMATION

Name: ____________________

School Telephone: ____________________

SHIP TO
School: ____________________
Address: ____________________
City: ____________________ Postal Code: __________

PAYMENT
☐ by credit card
VISA/MC Number: ____________________ Expiry Date: __________
Name on Card: ____________________
☐ enclosed cheque
☐ invoice school P.O. number: ____________________

Castle Rock Research Corp
#2340, 10180 – 101 Street, Edmonton, AB T5J 3S4 Tel: 780.448.9619 Fax: 780.426.3917
email: learn@castlerockresearch.com Toll-free: 1.800.840.6224
www.castlerockresearch.com

2006 (3)